THE SUBJECTIVE EXPERIENCE OF THE INDWELLING CHRIST

WITNESS LEE

Living Stream Ministry
Anaheim, CA

First Edition, December 2000.

ISBN 0-7363-1144-0

Published by

Living Stream Ministry
2431 W. La Palma Ave., Anaheim, CA 92801 U.S.A.
P. O. Box 2121, Anaheim, CA 92814 U.S.A.

Printed in the United States of America

01 02 03 04 05 06 / 10 9 8 7 6 5 4 3 2 1

CONTENTS

PREFACE

This book is a translation of messages given by Brother Witness Lee in the Chinese-speaking meetings in Anaheim, California on the Lord's Days between February and April of 1983. These messages were not reviewed by the speaker.

CHAPTER ONE

THE EXPERIENCE OF CHRIST AS LIFE

(1)

Scripture Reading: Col. 2:2; 3:4; Phil. 1:19-21

THE MYSTERY OF GOD—CHRIST

In Colossians 2 Paul told the Colossians that he wanted them to know how great a struggle he had for them and for those who had not seen his face, that their hearts might be comforted and that they might be knit together in love and unto all the riches of the full assurance of understanding, unto the full knowledge of the mystery of God, Christ (vv. 1-2). Here, *the mystery of God, Christ* literally means that God is difficult to understand and comprehend and therefore is a mystery, but Christ is the explanation, expression, and manifestation of the mysterious God. Thus, Christ is the mystery of God. When one sees Christ, one sees God and knows God. When the Lord Jesus was living on earth, He was full of love, grace, forbearance, meekness, and authority. Although we always have the desire to care for others and love our children, relatives, friends, brothers, and sisters, we are unable to do it. However, Christ is not like us. We desire to love, yet we are unable to love. Yet, Christ not only has love, but He is also able to love. With Him nothing is impossible; He can do all things. He is able to meet the needs of anyone. If you are sick, He can heal you; if you are deadened, He can enliven you; if you are hungry, He can feed you and five thousand others with five loaves and two fish. All His acts reveal all the fullness of the Godhead to the uttermost. Therefore, you can see God in Christ.

The literal meaning of the phrase *the mystery of God, Christ* appears to be very simple. Yet, according to the Bible, what this phrase implies is not so simple; rather, it includes a great many things that are beyond human imagination and comprehension. For example, a person who has received little education and has only a little knowledge may be able to recognize and read almost all the words in the newspaper, but he still does not understand what he has read. On the contrary, a knowledgeable person can tell what the end of the story will be by simply reading the opening lines and can know the content of a whole line by simply reading the first few words. Since he has been equipped with the knowledge of the subject matter, it is very easy for him to comprehend when he reads it. The same is true in reading the Bible. If our mind does not have the divine concept, regardless of how hard we try in our reading, we cannot receive the divine revelation. Eventually, what we receive in our reading is actually what we already have in our natural concept. For example, the Bible says, "Husbands, love your wives" (Eph. 5:25a). Every wife who comes across this verse would exclaim in her heart, "Amen! The Bible is really good and it is so right!" Why? The reason is that since the day she got married, she has earnestly hoped that her husband will love her. However, every husband who is provoked daily by his wife responds with an "amen" when he comes across the verse that says, "Wives, be subject to your own husbands" (v. 22). He understands this matter immediately because this is exactly what he expects of his wife. Actually, the book of Ephesians is filled with many high revelations and profound truths, yet we are unable to take them in.

THE REVELATION AND EXPERIENCE OF CHRIST

The high revelations and profound truths in the Bible are fundamentally non-existent in our natural concept. Our natural concept does not have this knowledge or this vocabulary; therefore, in our Bible reading we can understand only the superficial meaning of the words but not their intrinsic significance, much less understand the hidden mystery.

Colossians 2:2 speaks of "the mystery of God, Christ,"

referring first of all to Christ as the mystery of God being in us as our life (3:4). In the Scriptures, the book of Colossians is on the objective truth concerning Christ, while the book of Philippians is on the subjective experience of Christ. Colossians pulls open the heavenly veil to show us who Christ is and what Christ is. In Colossians 1 more than ten items concerning Christ are mentioned. The most important ones are Christ being the allotted portion of the saints (v. 12), Christ being the image of the invisible God (v. 15a), Christ being the Firstborn of all creation (v. 15b), and Christ being the first One in resurrection and in the new creation (v. 18). After speaking about who Christ is in chapter one, Paul goes on in chapter two to give Christ an aggregate title by saying that Christ is the mystery of God. Christ as the mystery of God is an aggregate title, just like the sum total in arithmetic. Christ is the mystery of God, and in this mystery many items are included. Then in chapter three, Paul says that this Christ, the mystery of God, is our life. This is Colossians, a book that reveals the truth concerning Christ.

The Bible is complete and covers all aspects. Not only does it speak about truth and revelation, but it also refers to the experience. Not only does it have the book of Colossians with the revelation of Christ, but it also has the book of Philippians with the experience of Christ. Not only does Paul tell us in Colossians that Christ is our life, but he also tells us in Philippians that Christ is our experience of life. The entire book of Philippians is filled with the experience of Christ.

THE MANIFESTATION
OF THE DIVINE CHARACTERISTICS THROUGH
ALL THE CREATED THINGS IN THE UNIVERSE

Romans 1:20 says, "For the invisible things of Him, both His eternal power and divine characteristics, have been clearly seen since the creation of the world." Here *divine characteristics* denotes the special features, the characteristics, as the outward manifestations of God's nature or substance which can be seen and appreciated by men. If you want to know God, just look at the universe with all the created things because the entire universe expresses the divine characteristics. When you see that the universe is full of light, you know that God is light; the universe is beautiful, so God is a God of beauty; the universe is full of vitality, so God is brimming with life; the universe is orderly with the heavenly bodies revolving in their proper orbits, so God is orderly and without confusion. Therefore, you know the characteristics of what God is through the manifestations of all the created things in the universe. Although knowledgeable people may know God as the Creator of the universe by observing the universe itself, they do not truly know who God is and what the Godhead is because their knowledge of God is merely according to the outward expression of the universe.

CHRIST AS THE EXPRESSION
OF THE GODHEAD

Who is this God with the Godhead? This needs to be explained and expressed by the Lord Jesus Christ. When the Lord Jesus came, He did not just show us the manifested characteristics of God, but even more He fully declared God Himself with the Godhead. This is because all the fullness of the Godhead dwelt in this incarnated Jesus bodily (Col. 2:9). God was the Word in eternity past (John 1:1). Although He had the fullness of the Godhead, to the naked eye this Godhead is not concrete, not "bodily." It was not until the time when the Word became flesh as Jesus of Nazareth, who lived on the earth among men, that the Godhead was manifested in Him bodily. Before God became flesh, He was the Word without a bodily form; when He became flesh, He assumed a bodily form. Christ is the mystery of God, the embodiment of God, because all the fullness of the Godhead dwells in Him bodily.

CHRIST'S BECOMING
THE SPIRIT TO BE OUR LIFE

Colossians 3:4 says, "Christ our life." Here it says that Christ is our life; it does not say that Christ is to be our life. It may sound better in Chinese to say that we experience Christ to be our life, but this utterance is not accurate. The accurate way is to say that we experience Christ as our life. The book of Colossians covers the matter of Christ as our life in the aspect of truth. Therefore, there is the need for the book of Philippians to go on to tell us how Christ is our life and how we can experience this Christ as our life.

Philippians 1:19 says, "Through...the Spirit of Jesus Christ." The Spirit of Jesus Christ is Jesus Christ. To God, Christ is His mystery; to us, Christ is the Spirit. The mystery of God, Christ, reaches us as the Spirit. *The Spirit of Jesus Christ* does not mean that Christ is one person and the Spirit is another person. In Greek, the expression *the Spirit of Jesus Christ* means that *the Spirit* is *Jesus Christ;* hence, the Spirit of Jesus Christ is Jesus Christ. Similarly, 2 Corinthians 3:17 says, "And the Lord is the Spirit; and where the Spirit of the Lord is, there is freedom." The first part of the verse says, "The Lord is the Spirit," and the latter part says, "The Spirit of the Lord." If you do not understand the spiritual significance of this verse, or your study of the original text is inadequate, you will think that the two statements contradict one another. The first part says, "The Lord is the Spirit," meaning that the Lord and the Spirit are one; then the verse goes on to say, "The Spirit of the Lord," seemingly implying that the Lord and the Spirit have become two entities. Actually it is not so. "The Lord is the Spirit; and where the Spirit of the Lord is, there is..." shows good sentence construction. In contrast, it is neither smooth nor grammatically correct to say, "The Lord is the Spirit where there is...." Furthermore, in verse 18b Paul also says that we "are being transformed...even as from the Lord Spirit." This proves that the Lord and the Spirit are one. The compound title *the Lord Spirit* does not mean that the Lord is one person and the Spirit is another person. *The Lord Spirit* is one person, not two. This is just like the compound title *the Father God,* indicating that God and the Father are one person, not two.

In order to be our life Christ had to become the Spirit, and indeed He has become the Spirit. "The last Adam became a life-giving Spirit" (1 Cor. 15:45b). Jesus became flesh, lived on the earth for thirty-three and a half years, died on the cross, and resurrected; in resurrection He became the life-giving

Spirit. Many Christians get lost here because they do not have the light.

The Lord Jesus was conceived of the Holy Spirit and was born of the virgin Mary with a body which was physical and belonged to the old creation. He lived on the earth for thirty-three and a half years and was crucified, but God raised Him from the dead. After passing through the process of death and resurrection, His body, which was of the old creation and physical, became a resurrected and spiritual body. This matter is clearly explained in 1 Corinthians 15. Through resurrection the body of the old creation which the Lord Jesus had put on was brought into the Spirit. Therefore, after His resurrection His body became a spiritual body. Thus, today Christ, who is the Spirit, is our life.

THE SPIRIT OF JESUS CHRIST
AS OUR SALVATION

Philippians 1:19 says, "For me this will turn out to salvation through...the bountiful supply of the Spirit of Jesus Christ." Regardless of our circumstances, the life-giving Spirit becomes our salvation through His bountiful supply. For example, if a man falls into the water, I can save him by dragging him out of the water. This kind of salvation merely delivers him from drowning; he does not gain me. He is saved, but he does not gain me as his salvation. What this verse means is that when a brother is in the midst of afflictions, because the Spirit of the Lord is in him, he is strengthened when he calls, "O Lord!" The more he calls, the more strengthened he is. Eventually when he is filled by the Holy Spirit, he is strengthened and empowered to overcome the oppression of afflictions. In this way the Lord becomes his salvation in him. Here you see that this brother is not only saved, but even more he has experienced the Spirit in him as his salvation. Many Christians, when reading this word, "for me this will turn out to salvation," understand it as an objective salvation. However, the Spirit of Jesus Christ turning out to be our salvation is subjective. Not only does He save us outwardly, but even more He becomes our salvation inwardly.

Christ in us becoming our salvation can be likened to the

life in our body being our daily salvation. For example, if your feet get trapped in the mud and if you are a person made of wood, a lifeless person, or you are a weakling, then you need others to pull you out of the mud. But as long as you are a living person with the power of life within you, the life in you will enable you to extricate your feet from the mud. Thus, the life in your body is your salvation. When medical doctors diagnose illnesses, they invariably tell patients that medicine helps cure an illness, but the real cure to someone's illness is the life in the body. If your physical life is healthy and strong, it cures you every day until your body fully recuperates. Thus, the life in your body is your salvation; this is not an objective, outward salvation, but rather a subjective, inward salvation. The Lord Jesus has become the Spirit of life in our spirit as our subjective salvation.

Philippians 1:20 says, "As always, even now Christ will be magnified in my body, whether through life or through death." Although the Lord Jesus as the Spirit indwelling our spirit is abstract, impalpable, and invisible, He is indeed saving us inwardly. The Lord Jesus has become the life-giving Spirit as our life and our salvation within us.

THE EXPERIENCE OF CHRIST'S SALVATION IN OUR HUMAN SPIRIT

Christ has become the life-giving Spirit as the life and life supply in our spirit. Therefore, we must live in our spirit to experience the salvation and the bountiful supply of the Spirit. Man has a three-layer constitution: the outermost layer is the body; within the body is the second layer, which is the soul; and within the soul is the third layer, which is the spirit. Today Christ is the Spirit, and within us we also have a spirit; therefore, we can experience Him. The two spirits—the Lord's Spirit and our spirit—are mingled and have fellowship with one another. This may be compared to metal conducting electricity. If we sin, an insulation comes between us and the Lord and then the "electricity" cannot pass through. At such a time we need to open up to Him in our spirit to repent and confess our sins. In this way the barrier of sin is removed; immediately we can have fellowship with the Lord Spirit and once again experience His salvation within us. Then the Lord Jesus is no longer a doctrine to us but a reality. As the Spirit, He now indwells our spirit so that we can daily experience Him as our salvation.

ONE PROBLEM—BEING ACCUSTOMED TO LIVING ACCORDING TO THE SOUL AND NOT ACCORDING TO THE SPIRIT

Although we have a spirit, do we live by this spirit in our daily life? This is our problem. Indeed, we have the spirit in us, yet we do not live according to the spirit. We are accustomed to living according to our soul in our daily life. We delight in and are accustomed to using our mind to consider, our emotion to love or to hate, and our will to decide. Every day we live according to our soul instead of according to the spirit within us. Before you were saved, you spoke recklessly and you lied. But now that you have repented and believed in the Lord, you realize that you should behave differently. Therefore, you do not commit outward sins and you do not lie. Nevertheless, just as your lying was of yourself, now your not lying is also of yourself; formerly your reckless behavior was of yourself, but now your proper behavior is also of yourself. You are not living according to the spirit but according to yourself. Consequently, although the Lord Jesus lives in your spirit, He is securely confined and restricted in you; you do not allow Him to live out through you. Instead, you are still living out your old habits and your old self.

Old habits are very difficult to change. Let me tell you a true story. In my early years in my hometown, Chefoo, there were electric lamps and telephones, but only very few people had them installed in their homes. Whenever we came home after dark, we would look for a match to light the kerosene lamp; we did this every day such that it became our habit. In 1939 my house finally had electric lamps. However, during the first couple of months, when I went home at the end of a busy day and noticed the room was dark, I would still spontaneously look for a match to light the kerosene lamp. My children would laugh at me. This is also the story of our daily life. Our speaking and our thoughts can be likened to lighting the kerosene lamp. The kerosene lamp is our self, whereas the electric lamp is the Spirit. Although we have the electric lamp installed in us from heaven, we are still controlled by our old habit. Instead of appropriating the electric lamp by turning on the switch, our spirit, we light up our kerosene lamp. Not using what one already has is tantamount to not having that thing at all. As believers, we have the Lord Jesus in our spirit, but our problem is that we do not use our spirit. We are accustomed to living according to the soul and not according to the spirit.

TO LIVE BEING CHRIST

Paul was a good pattern of one who lived according to the spirit, one who lived Christ. He always allowed Christ to be magnified in his body under any circumstances, whether smooth or rough, good or bad, whether through life or through death (Phil. 1:20b). What does this mean? This means that he ignored his mind, emotion, and will but cared only for the spirit within him by always opening up to the spirit. In this way Christ was lived out through him and was magnified in his body. First Christ entered into him, and then Christ was lived out from him. Christ was lived out and thus magnified. As a result, he could say, "For to me, to live is Christ" (v. 21a). When Paul lived, his living was Christ; this was his experience. This is why I want to speak to you something concerning our experience. Ever since I spoke about living Christ three or four years ago, I have often been asked this question: What is it to live Christ? We coined the phrase *live Christ*. Most Christians would say *live by Christ*, but this kind of utterance is not adequate. The word *living* in the phrase *living Christ* is a verb not an adjective. To live Christ means to live out Christ; therefore, to live is Christ.

LIVING CHRIST IN OUR DAILY LIFE

Recently someone also asked me, "How do I live Christ?" I will give a general answer to this question. First of all, let us see the experience of Christians in living Christ. Many Christians live according to themselves in their daily life. When it is time to go to the meeting, a Christian reminds himself, "I am going to the meeting now, so I have to exercise my spirit." Then he may have a little prayer to ask the Lord to bless the meeting. His wife would also remind him, "You always speak in haste. It is all right to speak hastily at the dinner table, but at the meeting you should be more cautious!" Thus, at the meeting he tries to be cautious and prays to the Lord, "O Lord, touch me by Your Spirit." Then when he is inspired, he says, "O Lord! Indeed You are my life!" This is one who lives Christ only during the meetings. Another one may live Christ in another way: A wife, for example, may have been bothering her husband for the past few days, or a husband may have been showing his displeasure towards his wife, and the situation has become unbearable, and this one is compelled to turn to the Lord and say, "O Lord, I am in fear and trembling simply because I am afraid that I will lose my temper and get into an exchange of words or even a fight. I want to live by You in fear and trembling." This is one who lives Christ only in times of difficulties. These examples prove that you do not live Christ when there are no meetings or difficulties. In our daily life, we all live ourselves instead of Christ. We live Christ only when it is time to go to the meetings or when we need to depend on Him in the midst of difficulties. This is the true situation of our daily living.

Brothers and sisters, we have to go against our habits. We should not wait to live Christ until we go to the meetings, speak in the meetings, or encounter difficult situations and persecutions. Rather, in our daily life, towards our wife, our children, or anyone, we should live and walk according to the spirit and not according to the soul, including the mind, emotion, and will. This is to live Christ in our daily living.

THE DIFFERENCE BETWEEN LIVING CHRIST AND ADHERING TO RELIGION

If a Christian waits until he is in a meeting to act like he is living Christ, then that is to have a true, formal, first-class religion. To be in a religion is to perform a kind of life in the meetings that is different from one's daily life. If you do not live Christ in your daily life, yet you try to perform something when you go to the so-called Sunday worship, that is religion.

Today the Lord does not want religion; what He wants is for us to live Christ whether in our daily life or in the meetings.

Today the Lord is in our spirit as our life. Therefore, we must exercise our spirit daily that Christ may be lived out through us. Just as I speak in the spirit in the meetings before the elders, so I also speak in the spirit at the family dinner table to my wife and children. Every day I live and walk according to the spirit. Then this is not religion but a spiritual living. This is the kind of living we ought to have; this is to live Christ. By this we experience the bountiful supply of the Spirit of Jesus Christ to be our salvation in all things. The indwelling Spirit with the bountiful supply will save us from the old creation and from the living that is of the old creation. If we live by and according to the spirit in all things, including big things and small things, and not just only in the meetings, then we have Christ instead of religion. We need to see that today we are in the Lord's recovery, not in religion. Therefore, we need to live Christ and not adhere to religion.

THE WAY OF SPIRITUAL LIVING— WALKING ACCORDING TO THE SPIRIT

How can we have such a spiritual living? The secret lies in our Savior, the Lord Jesus Christ. He is our God, our Creator, our Redeemer, our Savior, and the Lord of all, but today He has become the life-giving Spirit dwelling in us in a true and living way to be our life. Therefore, we should not speak, behave, live, or move according to our soul but according to our spirit. Moreover, we should remain in our spirit. The spirit in us is living and sensitive; we must exercise and learn to live and walk according to the sense of the spirit every time and everywhere. Moreover, we should establish a life of living Christ. Then we can say as Paul said, "For to me, to live is Christ."

CHAPTER TWO

THE EXPERIENCE OF CHRIST AS LIFE

(2)

Scripture Reading: Col. 2:2, 9; 3:4; Phil. 1:19-21a

Prayer: Lord, we thank You. You are our God and our Lord, and yet You became the life-giving Spirit to dwell in us as our life and everything. Lord, we are a group of people who can testify that we receive Your grace daily and enjoy Your presence. You speak to us every day from within, and You live in us as the strength of our practical living. Lord, we thank You all the more that You lead us in our daily living to take the pathway ahead. We beseech You to draw more people to hear Your gospel and receive You as life. We truly long for more people to be saved and to know You as the true and living God as well as the Lord who gives life that they may receive You as life.

Lord, we also ask that You cleanse us with Your precious blood that we may be well pleasing to You, have the anointing and the light of life, and be full of the comfort and encouragement of life within. Lord, we look to You to give us grace that we may live You and experience You daily to become one spirit with You, so that whenever we come together, we will be full of the experiences of You to be Your living testimony. May You receive our worship and exaltation. We give You all the glory and adoration. Amen.

ALL THINGS IN THE UNIVERSE AND
THE EXPERIENCE OF MAN
PROVING THE EXISTENCE OF GOD

In Colossians 2:2b we see that the mystery of God is

Christ. Because Christ is the explanation, manifestation, and expression of God, Christ is God's mystery. We also see in verse 9 that all the fullness of the Godhead dwells in Christ bodily. The Godhead is just God Himself, the very Creator whom we worship. The Godhead of this One dwells in Christ bodily. Therefore, Christ is the embodiment of God.

God is mysterious, but He is also very real. We can prove His existence from the principles of science, physics, physiology, and all things in the universe. Tens of thousands of Christians can also prove the existence of God from the experiences they have in their daily living. Although God is mysterious and invisible, man cannot say that there is no God just because he does not see Him. This is because invisible things are not necessarily nonexistent. Take electricity as an example. No one has seen electricity, and even those who specialize in electricity cannot pinpoint exactly where electricity is. What is seen are simply some manifestations of electricity. However, the existence of electricity is undeniable because everyone has used electricity. The specialists also tell us that there are electrical waves in the air. The term *electrical waves* indicates that there is energy in the air that is transmitted by the phenomenon of waves. Although electrical experts know that it is so, they do not know why it is so. Even though we do not understand it, if we tune a radio to the right frequency, the waves in the air will transmit the music to us.

Another example is our physical life, which is also abstract. Even the best biologists and the most brilliant doctors today have no way of showing us life. Although man's physical life is invisible, it truly exists. Furthermore, we may say that a certain person has an evil heart. This heart is not the biological heart referred to in medicine, but the psychological heart referred to in psychology. The Bible also says that the heart of men is deceitful above all things, wicked to the uttermost, and even incurable (Jer. 17:9). The heart here also refers to the psychological heart. We all know that the physical, biological heart in man is our human heart, but no one knows where the psychological heart is located. These examples prove that we cannot say that something does not exist just because we do not see it. As a mystery, God is invisible to our physical eyes; however, through all things in the universe and our experience, we know that God exists.

THE THREEFOLD NEED
OF THE TRIPARTITE MAN

The Bible tells us that man is composed of three parts. Apart from the body, man also has a soul; moreover, there is a spirit within the soul. Man's soul and spirit are both mysteries. It is interesting how the ancient Chinese formed these Chinese characters for *soul* and *spirit*. *Soul* belongs to the group of characters with *demon* as a radical, while *spirit* belongs to the group of characters with *rain* as a radical, which is also where the character *electricity* belongs. This is a hint that the spirit is as wonderful as electricity, which is invisible yet very real. If a man would carefully recall his past with all his experiences in a quiet and humble way, he will surely discover that there is a spirit within him.

We also know that when a person satisfies his physical needs for food, clothing, shelter, and transportation, he still does not feel satisfied within. Thus, he looks for various kinds of entertainment and amusement to satisfy his need. For example, admiring artistic works, listening to music, reading books, watching television and movies, and other matters are all for the entertainment of the soul. In Greek, the words for *soul* and *psychology* come from the same root word *psuche*. Therefore, the soul is the psychological part referred to in psychology, which is also what we often refer to as the metaphysical things, things that are invisible and without bodily form.

However, a person may have no lack in food, clothing, shelter, and transportation; he may have enjoyed every possible kind of entertainment and amusement. He may have achieved success and acquired fame, and he may have many children and grandchildren. Yet when he lies down to rest in the silence of the night, his deepest part often has a kind of bored and empty feeling. He still feels that human life is tasteless. Deep within him there is still a big void which cannot be filled, so he still has no satisfaction. This is the real condition of many people in the world. This empty part in the depths of man is what the Bible calls the human spirit. The hole, the void, in the deepest part of men is something that cannot be filled by any person, thing, or matter in the world. This is a sign of the hunger and thirst of the human spirit. In the deepest part of man, in man's spirit, there is truly a need which cannot be satisfied by any physical or psychological thing in the world.

THE BIRTH OF RELIGION

Throughout the ages, due to the fact that the need within man's spirit cannot be satisfied by anything in the world, religion was then invented. We all know that today there are five great religions in the world: Confucianism, Buddhism, Taoism, Mohammedanism, and the Judeo-Christian religion. Confucianism, which is composed of the teachings of Confucius, teaches people about ethics and morality but not the worship of God. Therefore, strictly speaking, it cannot be considered a religion. Buddhism, which was founded by Sakyamuni, does not even speak of the true God. It talks only about the wheel of reincarnation and meditation to become Buddha, and it also teaches people to practice abstinence, to do good, and to worship the clay statues of Buddha. Therefore, strictly speaking, it cannot be considered a religion either. Taoism teaches profound and mysterious thoughts, transcendence from worldliness, and self-cultivation to obtain immortality. It is merely an empty philosophy, so it cannot be considered a religion either. Mohammedanism, which is also called Islam, teaches people to worship the God who created the universe and not to worship idols; hence, it can be considered a religion. However, the Koran, the sacred book of the Moslems, was written by copying from and making changes to the Holy Scriptures of Judaism and Christianity; it is altogether a deviation from the biblical truths. Hence, Mohammedanism cannot be considered an orthodox religion.

The Judeo-Christian religion is composed of Judaism and Christianity. The Holy Bible of this religion teaches men to worship the unique true God, Jehovah, and declares Jesus Christ as King of kings and Lord of lords. None of the founders of religions or the great philosophers dared to proclaim himself as the Lord. Only the Bible tells us that there is a true God in the universe, and that He is the Lord, the Creator, and the sovereign One in the universe. The Old Testament says that Jehovah God is the Creator of all things; moreover, the New Testament says that Jesus Christ is the Lord of all (Acts 10:36). We all know that this year is A.D. 1983, which is counting from the year that Jesus Christ was born. Today all the countries in this world, including the atheistic communist countries, use a calendar based on the year of the birth of Jesus Christ. Logically speaking, the calendar a country uses indicates the one to whom this country belongs. Today all the countries of the world use the calendar of Jesus Christ as their calendar. This tells us that all the countries of the world belong to Jesus Christ. All men under heaven use the calendar of Jesus Christ as their calendar, so Jesus Christ is the Lord of all men of the world.

GOD BEING
THE UNIQUE SATISFACTION TO MAN

The need within the spirit of man cannot be satisfied by wealth and fame, nor by entertainment and amusement, nor by the religions invented by men. Man is a vessel created by God with the purpose of containing God Himself. Hence, man can have the real satisfaction within only by receiving his Creator as his life and content. You can sincerely cry out from deep within, saying, "O God, if You are real, I pray that You would cause me to know You and receive You. I need You. Although I have tasted the things of this world, I am still not satisfied within. I want to gain You as my satisfaction." When you call in this way, you will experience an indescribable joy within, and sometimes you will even be so joyful that you shed tears. Then the sense of emptiness deep within you will vanish. Nothing else can satisfy the need in our spirit, nor can anything else quench the thirst in our spirit; only God can. This is like a man walking in the wilderness or desert. When he is thirsty, you cannot quench his thirst by giving him gold coins or diamonds; only a cup of water can satisfy his need. Our God, our Lord, is the cup of water that man needs for his inner thirst. Only God, who is the living water, can quench the thirst in man's spirit (John 4:10, 14; 7:37-38).

If man wants to verify the existence of God in the universe, he can do that simply by touching the need in his spirit. In this universe, only this God can truly satisfy man's inner need. When a person calls on God, the need in his spirit is satisfied. This is neither an imaginary perception nor a superstitious belief. A person may call on Confucius again and again, yet he will not have any feeling within him. However, at any time and in any place, if a man sincerely cries out from the depths of his heart, "O Lord Jesus, I believe in You," he will have a sense within and he will obtain the reality. This reality within him will not only make him joyful and satisfied, but it will also change his behavior and his life. This kind of change is not out of man's exhortation and teachings; it is produced spontaneously from within.

We cannot contact God with our body or by our mental consideration because God is Spirit. If we want to contact God, we must use our spirit (John 4:24) because the human spirit is the organ for man to contact God. This may be compared to the receiver in a radio, which is the part that receives the radio waves in the air. Our God is the Lord who created all things in the universe. One day He became flesh to be a man, whose name was Jesus, and lived on the earth for thirty-three and a half years. Then He was crucified on the cross, and by the shedding of His precious blood He accomplished redemption for our sins and became our Redeemer. Moreover, He resurrected from the dead and became a life-giving Spirit. This life-giving Spirit is omnipresent. Although He is invisible and intangible, we can touch Him by calling on the name of the Lord (Rom. 10:8-9). When we call on the name of the Lord Jesus, we receive the Lord Jesus because the Lord's name is just the Lord Himself. Furthermore, after the Lord Jesus resurrected from the dead, He became the life-giving Spirit, so when we call on the Lord's name, this Spirit enters into our spirit to regenerate and save us. Then the Lord Jesus becomes our life and everything to us in our spirit and thus becomes the real satisfaction within us.

CHRIST BEING A LIVING PERSON
IN HIS BELIEVERS

A Christian is one who has Christ in him as life. When a person believes in Christ and Christ enters into the spirit of this one to be his life and his Savior, he becomes a Christian. The suffix -*ian* does not refer to a "disciple" but to a "man." Hence, a "Christian" is a "Christ-man." A "Christ-man" refers to a person who has Christ in him as his life and everything. This is not an empty noun or a doctrine, but a real experience. This Christ who lives inside us, the Christ-men, is the life-giving Spirit. He is the Lord as a person who lives in our spirit as our life to make us Christ-men.

Therefore, a Christ-man is not so simple because within the Christ-man there is Christ and there is also the natural self. There are two persons living together inside every Christ-man: one is the natural self and the other is Christ. Unlike a male and a female who are married to become a couple living together outwardly, these two persons live together within us. We all can testify that within us there are really two persons living together. In our daily living almost every day we have this story: When we want to do something, often this person who is in us, the Lord Jesus, does not agree. Hence, these two persons within us are in conflict. This kind of conflict was not there before we became Christ-men. For example, before the sisters believed in the Lord, when they saw the advertisement of a big sale in the newspaper, they immediately went to buy some items without any struggle. However, after you have been saved and have become a Christ-man, when you see an advertisement of a big sale and want to go and buy a dress that is on sale, there is Someone in you who says, "No." While you are on your way, He keeps saying, "No." When you enter into the main entrance of the department store, He still says, "No"; but you still do not pay attention to His disagreement, and so when you are about to buy the dress, He still says, "No," and keeps saying, "No," to the end. This "no" bothers you until you can no longer tolerate it, and you say, "If You say, 'no,' then let it be 'no.' I won't buy anymore." When you say this, He immediately calms down and you also feel comfortable. As you are in your car going home, you will be able to rejoice and say, "Amen, hallelujah! Lord Jesus, You are so lovely. I really love You."

However, sometimes because you like that dress so much and you also have a strong character, even though there is Someone in you who says, "No," you still bargain with Him, saying, "Lord, please allow me this time. I won't do it again." Then the Lord becomes quiet and remains silent, and you think that you can now buy the dress. However, after you have bought it, you are not able to pray and you have no joy; rather, you feel very bad. Originally, the dress was very lovely, but now you do not even dare look at it, because when you see it, you feel bad within. You feel bad when you put it aside, and you feel worse when you put it on. Then one day you give it to someone who is in need, and you immediately become joyful within. What is this story? This is a story of two persons living together. All these experiences tell us that the Christ within us is a living person.

Right now while I am here speaking a message to you, my whole being is very released because my outer man is not in conflict with the Lord within. The two persons are one, so my words have much light and much anointing. On the contrary, if my outer man has a problem with the Lord who is within me, and if I do not care for Him or love Him, yet I tell you that He is lovely and that we should love Him and obey Him, then this becomes acting. A false tone cannot fool people. If we truly live with Christ as two persons living together in oneness, we will have the anointing. When we pray, we can touch heaven, and we can also touch the spirit of others, ministering life and life supply to them.

CHRIST BECOMING
THE ALL-INCLUSIVE SPIRIT

The Bible explicitly says that the Lord Jesus, the God-man, has become the life-giving Spirit (1 Cor. 15:45b) to dwell in our spirit. Now He is the Spirit, the all-inclusive Spirit. Because the Lord Jesus is God, the Spirit has the element of God, and because He is also a man, the Spirit also has the element of man. He was on earth for thirty-three and a half years and lived the life of an ordinary man. Therefore, the

Spirit also has the element of the experiences of human life. He died on the cross and shed His blood for us to redeem us from our sins and terminate our old creation, flesh, lusts, natural being, and self, and then He also resurrected and ascended for us. Therefore, in the Spirit there are the elements of the effectiveness of His death, the power of His resurrection, and the glorification in His ascension. When we live together with Him, that is, when we live and move by the Spirit, unconsciously this Spirit annihilates, one by one, our flesh, natural man, disposition, and self, while at the same time He supplies us all our needs. This Spirit is like a tablet of medicine that contains various ingredients, including some that kill germs and others that supply nutrients. If a person would take this tablet regularly, it will kill the germs which should not be in the body, while at the same time it will supply the various nutrients that the human body lacks and thus cause the body to become stronger.

The Lord Jesus has already become the all-inclusive Spirit to dwell in our spirit. Hence, as long as we live by this spirit, our peculiarities, natural man, self, selfishness, and pride will be unknowingly annihilated and destroyed. This is not the work of self-cultivation but the result produced out of our growth in life through the daily transformation and renewing work carried out in us by the living Christ as the all-inclusive Spirit living in our spirit.

BEING ACCORDING TO THE SPIRIT AND LIVING CHRIST

The Bible tells us that the purpose of God in creating man is for man to contain Him and to express Him by living Him out. Hence, God does not want us to live by ourselves; rather, He wants us to live by Him. However, we have been accustomed to living by ourselves since our birth. Therefore, after we have been saved, although we have Christ as life within, we are still accustomed to living by ourselves. Formerly we lied and did evil things. Now after we have believed in the Lord, we know that we should be careful not to lie and do evil things, but our not lying or doing evil things by ourselves is still by ourselves and not by the Christ who lives in us.

When listening to the word, many Christians exercise their eyes and ears instead of their spirit, and their mind is full of criticism. Because they are so active in their soul, Christ is securely imprisoned in them and is unable to come out. When do people live by Christ? For some it is when they face great trouble and become completely helpless; for some it is when they are extremely sick and have nothing to rely on; and for some it is when they lose their job and cannot make a living anymore. Many of us have to wait until such a situation arises before we turn to our spirit and cry, "O Lord, have mercy on me." However, living Christ in this kind of way is not normal. We are Christ-men, not religious men. We should not wait until we pray in the meetings to live Christ, nor should we wait until we have a big problem before we call on the Lord and live Christ. To do that is too religious. We need to live together with Christ in our daily living, in whatever we do and in whatever place we may be. If we can live a spiritual life in this way every day, we will be those who live Christ. This is the thing that pleases Him most.

Christ-men not only have the God-created conscience, but all the more they have the Lord of life within them as life. Therefore, we should not be like the Chinese philosophers who practiced self-cultivation to develop the highest virtue. Rather, we need to let Christ live Himself out through us. To develop the highest virtue is like lighting the kerosene lamp as men did in the old days; however, since you are a man in the modern days who has electric lights installed in your house, you do not need the kerosene lamps anymore. We all have the Spirit within and we have all had the spiritual "electric lights" installed within us; hence, we no longer need to light the kerosene lamps. We only need to turn on the switch within to live by the Spirit. Furthermore, we should never turn it off after it has been turned on. In this way we will then be able to shine forth day and night and live Christ joyfully. In our daily living, in whatever circumstance, whether through life or through death, even as always Christ will be magnified in our body (Phil. 1:20). This is not to develop the highest virtue but to let Christ be lived out and magnified as always.

Philippians 1:21a says, "For to me, to live is Christ." For us to live is not morality or immorality but Christ. It is not a question of being moral or immoral, nor a question of having the highest virtue or not having the highest virtue, but a question of living Christ. How can it be that for us "to live is Christ"? It is by living and walking according to the Spirit within us. If the Spirit within us says, "No," we also say, "No"; if the Spirit within us says, "Yes," we then say, "Amen." This is what it means by "to live is Christ."

First Corinthians 6:17 says, "But he who is joined to the Lord is one spirit." Today we have already become one spirit with the Lord. Hence, in our dealings with our children, relatives, intimate friends, brothers and sisters, parents, neighbors, colleagues, or classmates, we need to walk according to the mingled spirit within us. We have already become one spirit with the Lord. Hence, wherever we may be, the Spirit will always be in us as our life. We need to live together with Christ in this Spirit to express Him. This is our spiritual living. Only in this way can we have peace and joy and the growth in life as well. This is to experience Christ as life.

CHAPTER THREE

THE INDWELLING CHRIST

Scripture Reading: John 14:16-20, 23; 15:4a; Rom. 8:9-11; Eph. 3:16-17

Prayer: O Lord, we worship You because You are our God, our Creator, and our Redeemer. Lord, we come together to Your word before You reverently. May You anoint us richly with Your Spirit and move within each one to shine forth the light of Your word, so that while we are reading, we may see the light and revelation and receive the supply of the Holy Spirit. Lord, we thank and praise You from deep within, because You died and resurrected for us and have become the life-giving Spirit, who not only is in heaven but also dwells in our spirit. Lord Jesus, we look to You from the depths of our being, expecting You to impart more of Yourself to us again and transfuse Yourself into us through Your words, which are spirit and are life. O Lord, we come here not only to hear Your words, but even more to receive Yourself, because Your very self is in Your words. Your words entering into us are just Yourself entering into us. Lord, may You open our mind, enlighten the eyes of our heart, and remove all our veils. May You sprinkle Your precious blood upon us once again to cleanse us so that because of this blood we may have a pure conscience and be at peace before You without any barrier or fear. Lord, it is such a glory and a blessing that we are able to contact You and have fellowship with You. May You give us a comforting word, a solid word, an encouraging word, a healing word, and a life-supplying word. Lord, every one of us has a need. You are the all-sufficient Lord. May You give us a sentence, or even just a few words, to meet each one's need. We really look to You to give us a living word.

Lord, we ask You to destroy Your enemy, who often troubles us. Destroy his power of darkness and even destroy his strongholds in our mind. We pray that You would eliminate any lukewarmness or hesitation within us so that our whole heart may incline toward You.

Lord, today is the morning of Your resurrection and the day of our salvation. May You gain us and gain more ground in each one of us. Lord, operate more and more among us that, with our spirits uplifted and burning, we may thank You, praise You, and worship You together. Your name is a victorious name. In this name we pray, and by this name we bind the strong man and plunder his house. May You gain all the glory this morning, and may Your enemy be put to shame. Amen!

THE LORD JESUS AS THE COMFORTER OUTSIDE HIS DISCIPLES WHILE HE WAS ON EARTH

In John 14:16 the Lord Jesus said, "I will ask the Father, and He will give you another Comforter." The Greek word for *Comforter* is difficult to translate because it is a very particular word; its anglicized form is *paraclete*. The word refers to one who is called to your side to wait on you, to take care of you, and to bear all your responsibilities. If you are sick, he is both the doctor and the nurse to take care of you. If you have a legal case, he is the lawyer to help you handle the case and go to court to represent you in the lawsuit. Moreover, if you encounter any problem in your daily life, he is your counselor. He can solve your problem, and you can pour out your heart to him and enjoy his kind protection. This Greek word implies a great deal. First John 2:1 says, "We have an Advocate with the Father, Jesus Christ the Righteous." This Advocate is our Comforter. The Greek word for *Advocate* is the same as that for *Comforter;* the two titles refer to the same One.

Originally, the Lord Jesus was God over all and the Creator of the universe (Rom. 9:5; John 1:3). One day He humbled Himself to become a man by being conceived and born of a virgin in a manger. He lived in the despised city of Nazareth and grew up in a poor carpenter's home. When He was thirty years old, He went out to preach the word, heal the sick, cast out demons, perform signs and wonders, and teach the truth. He was with His disciples for three and a half years and was very thoughtful of them. He knew their problems and was able to meet all their needs. Parents love their children, yet often they are unable to render any help to their children when their children have problems. The Lord Jesus, however, was not only kind and thoughtful but also omniscient and omnipotent. He lived, walked, ate, and drank with His disciples. He solved all their problems and ministered to all their needs. He was not only their Doctor and Nurse but also their Lawyer and Counselor. He was truly their Comforter.

THE LORD JESUS AS THE COMFORTER
INSIDE HIS DISCIPLES
AFTER HIS DEATH AND RESURRECTION

While the Lord Jesus was on the earth, He was with His disciples in an outward way for three and a half years; He was a tender, caring Comforter. However, after three and a half years, suddenly one day He told His disciples that He was going away from them and was going to Him who sent Him (John 16:5). The disciples were shocked by His word and felt sorrowful. Nevertheless, He told them not to be sorrowful, saying, "It is expedient for you that I go away" (v. 7). This was because, while at that time His physical presence with the disciples was wonderful, He could be among them only in an outward way since He was still in the flesh, limited by time and space. He could not be with His disciples if they were at the Sea of Galilee in the north while He was in the temple in Jerusalem to the south. Therefore, He had to go and have a change to become the life-giving Spirit. Thus, He would be able to enter into them to be with them at any time and in any place as the Comforter within them. For the disciples that would be His best presence.

The most precious result of our faith in Christ is that we receive Him into us. Although this is the pure and unadulterated yet mystical truth, it has been neglected by most Christians. They say that today Christ is sitting on the throne in heaven and that He does not dwell in His believers. The

Bible tells us, however, that today Christ is in heaven on the right hand of God but at the same time He also dwells in His believers (Rom. 8:34, 10). Our experience also confirms that Christ is indeed in us today. In those days the Lord Jesus was with His disciples and He walked, stayed, and lived with them, but He could not enter into them. Therefore, He had to go and have a change through death and resurrection; in His resurrection He would come back to enter into His disciples.

The Lord Jesus was with His disciples as a small Nazarene. Like a grain of wheat, He had nothing to be admired at outwardly, yet within Him there was the mystery of life, the riches of life, and the glory of life. First Corinthians 15 says that a grain bears a certain kind of body before it is sown and bears another kind of body after it grows (vv. 37-38). When the Lord Jesus was crucified and buried, that was His being sown into the soil. However, after a period of time, He came out of the tomb and was resurrected. In His resurrection He was different from before; He no longer appeared as a little man of Nazareth but rather became a man with another kind of body. The Bible tells us that in His resurrection the Lord was a pneumatic man with a body of glory. Furthermore, even though He was pneumatic, He was not abstract. On the evening of His resurrection, while His disciples gathered in a house with the doors tightly shut, suddenly the Lord came and stood in their midst. While they were in amazement, the Lord Jesus said to them, "Peace be to you." Then He appeared to them another time and said to Thomas, "Bring your finger here and see My hands, and bring your hand and put it into My side" (John 20:19-27). How wonderful! The Lord's body was spiritual, yet it could also be touched and handled.

The Lord Jesus still had a physical body after His death and resurrection. But even though He had a physical body, He was also pneumatic; this is marvelous. In the evening of His resurrection, when He came to the house where the disciples were meeting, instead of preaching to them, He said, "Peace be to you." And after He had said this, He breathed into them and said to them, "Receive the Holy Spirit." *Pneuma,* the Greek word for *Spirit,* may be rendered also as *wind* or *breath.* The Lord Jesus was resurrected as the Spirit, and this Spirit was the Holy Breath which He breathed into His disciples, yet He still possessed a spiritual body.

The Holy Spirit is the Holy Breath, and the Holy Breath is the Holy Spirit. When the Lord became the Holy Spirit, He became the Holy Breath. After the Lord Jesus breathed the Holy Breath into the disciples, and while they were in great amazement and rejoicing, He disappeared again. This was because at that time He had already entered into them. When He breathed into the disciples, He breathed the Spirit into them; this means that He breathed Himself into them. From that time onward, the disciples had a treasure abiding in them, a treasure that would never leave them again. Peter thought that the Lord was One who came and left suddenly. Therefore, when he did not see the return of the Lord after waiting for many days, he returned to his former profession and went fishing, and the rest of the disciples also went fishing with him at the Sea of Tiberias. However, that night they caught nothing. And as soon as the morning broke, the Lord stood on the shore and said to them, "You do not have any fish to eat, do you?" They answered Him, "No." Then the Lord told them to cast the net on the right side, and they caught a hundred and fifty-three large fish. Furthermore, the Lord had already prepared bread and fish on the shore to feed them (John 21:2-13). In this way, for forty days after His resurrection (Acts 1:3), the Lord sometimes appeared to His disciples and at other times hid Himself from them with the intention of training them to enjoy His invisible presence. The Comforter who was formerly outside the disciples could now enter into them to be the Comforter within them through the process of death and resurrection.

THE COMFORTER AS
THE INDWELLING SPIRIT OF REALITY

John 14:16-17a says, "And I will ask the Father, and He will give you another Comforter, that He may be with you forever, even the Spirit of reality." The Comforter is the Spirit of reality. Without the Spirit there is no reality and everything becomes doctrines in letter. Verse 17b goes on to say that "the world cannot receive" the Spirit of reality, "because it does not behold Him or know Him; but you know Him, because He abides with you and shall be in you." Before we were saved, we did not have the Spirit of reality, but after we have been saved, we have Him abiding in us. Sometimes He makes us happy, while other times He gives us trouble. For example, before you were saved, you did not have any uneasy feeling when you went to any department store to buy anything. However, after you have been saved, because the Spirit of reality dwells in you, sometimes when you want to buy something, He would not agree. If you disregard His feeling and buy it anyway, you will feel uneasy within and you will not be able to pray. This is proof that the Spirit is truly abiding in you.

Verse 18 says, "I will not leave you as orphans; I am coming to you." First, verse 17 says, "He abides with you," and then verse 18 says, "I will not leave you." The subject is changed from *He* to *I*. This means that *He* is *I*. "I will not leave you as orphans; I am coming to you." This coming is the coming of the Spirit of reality. The Spirit's coming is the Lord's coming. Moreover, verse 19 says, "Yet a little while and the world beholds Me no longer, but you behold Me; because I live, you also shall live." The Lord was going to die and be buried, so the world would behold Him no longer. However, the disciples beheld Him because He was resurrected. After His resurrection, He became the Spirit to enter into the disciples and live in them. Therefore, just as He lived, so they also lived. They lived together with Him.

Verse 20 says, "In that day you will know that I am in My Father, and you in Me, and I in you." This is truly a mystery! We are in the Lord, and the Lord is in the Father; so we are also in the Father. Furthermore, the Lord is in us, and because the Father and the Lord are one, the Father is also in us. The three—the Father, the Lord (the Son), and we—mutually dwell in one another. Hence, anyone who believes in the Lord Jesus has the Spirit of reality abiding in him. Thus, he is mingled with God and partakes of the divine nature (2 Pet. 1:4). We who are believers of the Lord Jesus become a peculiar people. Since we have the Spirit of the Lord in us as our supply, we are able to attain to all endurance and long-suffering with joy, enduring what others cannot endure (Col. 1:11). Sometimes we have been wronged, but we do not complain; other times we have been rebuked, but we are not angry. Rather, we give thanks and praise to the Lord in everything. This is the story of "you in Me, and I in you."

THE MUTUAL ABIDING
OF CHRIST AND HIS BELIEVERS

John 14:23 says, "Jesus answered and said to him, If anyone loves Me, he will keep My word, and My Father will love him, and We will come to him and make an abode with him." Verse 20 already indicates that "I [the Lord Jesus] am in My Father, and you in Me, and I in you." This means that the Lord Jesus abides in the Father, and we abide in the Lord Jesus, and the Lord Jesus abides in us. Thus, the Lord becomes our abode, and we become His abode. Moreover, He and the Father will come to us to make an abode with us. In 15:4a the Lord Jesus went on further to say, "Abide in Me and I in you."

John 14 speaks about the matter of mutual abiding in one way, while John 15 goes further and speaks about it in another way. Chapter fourteen says, "You in Me, and I in you" (v. 20); it also says, "If anyone loves Me,...We [My Father and I] will come to him and make an abode with him" (v. 23). Then chapter fifteen says, "Abide in Me and I in you" (v. 4a). Not only so, Romans 8:9 goes further to say that "the Spirit of God dwells in you." The Spirit of God here is the Spirit of Christ, even Christ Himself. Then Ephesians 3:17 goes even further to say that "Christ may make His home in your hearts." In Greek the word for *make...home* is different from the word for *dwells* in Romans 8 and from the word for *abide* in John 14 and 15. The word for *abide* in the Gospel of John is used in a general sense. The word for *dwells* in Romans is the verb form of the word for *house;* it means to inhabit as one's abode and is a stronger word than *abide.* To *make home* in Ephesians is even stronger than *dwells* in Romans; it means not only to inhabit but also to settle down in a dwelling, to make home by being deeply rooted. Christ not only dwells in us but also makes home in us, and He even settles down in us by being deeply rooted in our heart. The experience of believing in the Lord Jesus is a matter of changing residence. Before we believed in the Lord, we dwelt in Adam; when we believed in the Lord, we moved into Christ. In Adam, all we had were the fall, sin, darkness, and death; in Christ, we have transcendence, victory, light, and life. When we believe in the Lord Jesus, we move out of Adam into Christ; we no longer dwell in the old Adam but in Christ. Hallelujah, we are those who have changed our residence and have a new address!

THE LORD JESUS BECOMING OUR SALVATION THROUGH TEN GREAT STEPS

From the Bible we can see that the Lord Jesus became the salvation of those who believe in Him through ten great steps. He passed through these processes to become their salvation.

1. In Eternity Past

In eternity past the Lord Jesus was God (John 1:1). He is the God who is without beginning, self-existing, and ever-existing.

2. Incarnated

The Lord Jesus, the God who created the universe, was incarnated to become a man. In order to accomplish redemption, He was conceived of the Holy Spirit and born of a virgin, possessing both divinity and humanity.

3. Lived on the Earth

Through incarnation the Lord Jesus became a genuine man and grew up in a poor carpenter's home. He passed through human life, living and moving on the earth for thirty-three and a half years, in which He fully tasted the poverty of human life and experienced all its sufferings. At the age of thirty, He went forth to preach and work, extensively contacting different kinds of people. However, His words offended the Jews, the leaders in Judaism, and Caesar's agents in the Roman Empire. He indeed passed through all the things of human life on earth.

4. Crucified on the Cross

After living on the earth for thirty-three and a half years, He delivered Himself to the place of death and was crucified. He died for our sins and brought us and all things with Him to His death. His death is all-inclusive, not only redeeming us from our sins but also terminating all things of the old creation.

5. Resurrected

After His death and burial, the Lord Jesus was resurrected. In His incarnation He brought God into man; in His crucifixion He dealt with man's sins; in His resurrection He brought man into God. This was truly an earth-shaking event and the wonder of all wonders in the universe. By His coming and His going He brought God into man and man into God. In Him God and man converged and were mingled as one. At this point the mingling of God and man was accomplished. Redemption for sins was made, and all negative things in the universe were cleared away. On the first day of the week He was resurrected, and there was a germination in the universe. Furthermore, in His resurrection He became the life-giving Spirit (1 Cor. 15:45b) to enter into those who believe in Him that they may have the divine life and partake of the divine nature. God can enter into them, and they can enter into God. This is the effect of Jesus' death and resurrection.

6. Ascended to the Heavens

After His resurrection from death, the Lord ascended to the heavens. That was God ascending to the heavens with man. This is a tiding of great joy. There is a man sitting on God's throne of glory in heaven. This is truly a wonderful and glorious matter. He is sitting on the throne in heaven, having both God and man in Him. This One who has ascended to the heavens and is sitting on the throne is the Lord Jesus, in whom God and man converged.

7. Indwelling

It is such a One, the Lord Jesus, who comes into us to

indwell us when we believe in Him. At this point, we all have to shout with rejoicing because Christ is not only our Savior but also the glorious indwelling Christ. This resurrected Christ is the mingling of God and man. He passed through incarnation and crucifixion to become our Redeemer. Moreover, in His resurrection He became the life-giving Spirit to become our Savior. He also ascended to heaven and is now sitting there, having been made both Lord and Christ (Acts 2:36). As the King of kings and the Lord of lords, He has received authority and has been crowned with glory and honor. Yet such a One dwells in us! He not only abides in us but also dwells in us. Moreover, He is making home in our hearts. He is in us not only as our life but also as our person.

8. Coming Again

Not only so, Acts 1:11 says that the Lord Jesus will come again. At His coming again, we will be caught up to meet Him in the air and thus be always with Him (1 Thes. 4:17).

9. Reigning

At His coming again, the Lord Jesus will set up His kingdom on the earth to reign over the earth for a thousand years. It is not possible for man to rule the earth and make it a better place. At the end of the First World War the League of Nations was formed, yet the world did not become better. After the Second World War the United Nations was formed, yet the more the whole world tries to be united, the more divided it becomes. Only when the Lord Jesus reigns as King at His coming again can there be real peace on the earth.

10. In Eternity Future

Finally, after the thousand years, in eternity future the Lord Jesus will reign forever in the New Jerusalem.

THE KEY POINT IN ENJOYING CHRIST'S SALVATION

Today the key point, the most important point, in our enjoyment of Christ's salvation is the indwelling Christ. Christ has ascended to heaven, but at the same time He is also dwelling in us. On the one hand, He is in heaven interceding

for us as our great High Priest, our Advocate, to carry out
God's economy. On the other hand, He is the all-inclusive
indwelling Christ who dwells in us as our Comforter to be our
life and all of our supply.

The Lord Jesus was originally the Comforter outside of us,
but after His death and resurrection He became the Spirit of
reality to come into us to be the Comforter inside of us. This
indwelling Christ is our life and our person.

CHAPTER FOUR

CHRIST'S INDWELLING

Scripture Reading: Gen. 1:27; 2 Cor. 4:4b; Rom. 9:21, 23; 2 Cor. 4:6-7; John 14:20, 23; Eph. 3:16-17, 19

In the preceding chapter we saw the indwelling Christ—Christ as the indwelling One who lives in us. In this chapter we want to see Christ's indwelling. We want to know how this indwelling Christ lives in us and what this indwelling is all about.

CHRIST'S INDWELLING BEING REAL
AND INTIMATE THOUGH MYSTERIOUS

We know that Christ is truly a mystery, and His indwelling is even more a mystery. Even so, Christ's indwelling is very real and intimate because it is not something that takes place outside of us but rather something that transpires within us and is intimately related to us. Therefore, this is a very real and subjective matter.

MAN AS A CREATED VESSEL
TO CONTAIN CHRIST

Genesis 1:27 tells us that God created man in His own image. There is no other book in the universe that tells us in such a definite way that man was not only created by God but that he was also created in God's own image. Only the Bible tells us explicitly that man was created by God in His own image.

Man definitely did not evolve from something else. Rather, man was created by God in His own image. Who is God's image? The Bible tells us that Christ is the image of God. Second Corinthians 4:4b says, "Christ, who is the image of

God." Colossians 1:15 says that Christ as the Son of God's love "is the image of the invisible God." Therefore, when God created us in the beginning, He created us according to Christ. Romans 9:21 tells us that God created us and chose us that we might be vessels to contain Him. Hence, we were not only created according to the image of Christ, but we were also created as vessels instead of instruments. Vessels are different from instruments. Knives, axes, and saws are instruments for working, whereas glasses and tea cups are vessels for containing something. God did not create us as instruments to work for Him; instead, He created us as vessels to contain Him.

Based upon Genesis 1:27, Paul wrote Romans 9:21. He realized that in the beginning God created man with clay and that this man of clay is a vessel. However, this vessel is not for containing milk or water but the God of glory. Hence, in Romans 9:23 Paul said, "In order that He might make known the riches of His glory upon vessels of mercy, which He had before prepared unto glory." This glory denotes God Himself, because in Psalms and Jeremiah we are told that the children of Israel forsook their glory (Psa. 106:20; Jer. 2:11) instead of being told that they forsook their God. To forsake the glory is to forsake God, because God is glory. Without God, the universe and all that is in it has no glory. God is the source of all glory and splendor.

We are earthen vessels to contain God. When God comes into us, we become vessels of glory. Man was created by God to contain God. This concept cannot be found in any other book. Besides the Bible, there is no other book in the world that has such a record. Second Corinthians 4:6 says, "The God who said, Out of darkness light shall shine, is the One who shined in our hearts." This light is the expression of glory. Without glory, there is no brightness shining out, because light is the manifestation of glory. This glory is God, and the shining forth of light is the expression of God. God shines in our hearts by Himself as the light of glory. This is just like a camera. When the shutter is open, the image of the beautiful scene with beautiful flowers is exposed on the film through the entrance of light. We are a living camera created by God, and within us we have the film, which is our spirit. When you hear the gospel of the Lord, and if you believe Him in your heart and call upon His name with your mouth, you are a camera with an open shutter, and the film within you is readily exposed to the light. This exposure is everlasting and continuous. I was exposed to this light on an afternoon fifty-eight years ago. This exposure has been going on in me for all these years without ceasing, and it cannot be erased. Every Christian has this kind of experience.

Our spirit is the film concealed in our heart. When the glory of the Lord shines into our heart, our spirit is exposed to the light. At this time Christ as the treasure comes into us. Following verse 6, therefore, 2 Corinthians 4:7 says, "But we have this treasure in earthen vessels." This treasure is the indwelling Christ who enters into us through the light. Our spirit is exposed to the light when we are touched as we hear the gospel of the Lord, testify for the Lord, read the Word, or study spiritual books. Although we may not be aware of it, this exposure is still working within us. Sometimes we are busy with outward affairs, and we think that the light is fading. Actually, the light to which we have been exposed still remains in us.

For that one time of exposure to the light, we not only thank God for His mercy and praise Him for His love today, but in the millennial kingdom and in eternity we will still offer thanksgiving to Him. This exposure to the light is exceedingly precious. On that day fifty-eight years ago the Lord Jesus caused me to be exposed to the light, and thus I have Him in me as the treasure. Now this treasure is in me, an earthen vessel. This is not a small thing because this is Christ's indwelling. This treasure in us is the Lord Jesus, who is living and constantly speaking. He is a living treasure. As such, when He comes into us, He always bothers us. It is easy for us to put a table in our house. All we need to do is find a suitable place in the house and put the table there. But if we bring a vivacious child into our house, he will bring us many problems. This treasure—the Lord Jesus—in us is living and troublesome. In spite of this, we still love Him. He is greater and stronger than we are, and He is never careless. He is full of patience and is not prone to anger. Regardless of how we treat Him, He is not angered. Even when we reject Him, He does not leave us. This is the story of Christ's indwelling.

CHRIST'S MAKING HIS HOME

Some Christians know that Christ's indwelling is a mystery, but they do not truly understand it. After His resurrection, the Lord Jesus became the life-giving Spirit (1 Cor. 15:45b) to dwell in the spirit of those who believe in Him. This is a clear revelation in the Bible. Second Timothy 4:22 says, "The Lord be with your spirit," and Romans 8:16 says, "The Spirit Himself witnesses with our spirit that we are children of God." These verses show us that the Spirit is in our spirit and is mingled with our spirit so that the two spirits have become one. Today we, the saved ones, are one spirit with the Lord. The New Testament clearly speaks about this, although it is a mystery.

Through my many years of studying the Word, I can tell you that the most crucial items in the New Testament are the indwelling Christ and Christ's indwelling. The New Testament not only speaks about a mysterious person, Christ, but it also speaks about one thing concerning this mysterious person, that is, that Christ indwells His believers. Ephesians 3:16, 17, and 19 say that Paul prayed for us that God would grant us, according to the riches of His glory, to be strengthened with power through His Spirit into the inner man. We have an outer man and an inner man. Our inner man is our regenerated spirit. God will grant us, according to the riches of His glory, to be strengthened with power through His Spirit into the inner man, which is our regenerated spirit. The Greek word for *power* is a very strong word and is equivalent to the English word *dynamo*, denoting the energizing or motivating power of a generator. God strengthens us into the inner man with power through His Spirit according to the riches of His glory that Christ may make His home in our hearts through faith.

Although Christ is in us and has shined into us, He has not yet made His home in our hearts. What does it mean to make home? It means that after arranging everything properly,

He settles down. It is through faith and not by sight that Christ is making His home in our hearts. The result is that we are filled unto all the fullness of God. The fullness of God is the expression of the overflow of God. When Christ makes His home in us, we are filled with God and are full of the glory of God. As a result, we who are earthen vessels, vessels of clay, become vessels of glory. We are filled and saturated with all the riches of God so that we are full of God within and without. Then we will be as stanza 8 of *Hymns,* #489 says, "And everywhere be Thee [Christ] and God." Because the Spirit of Christ has saturated and permeated our entire being, everywhere in our being there is Christ, and everywhere there is God. In this way we become vessels of glory.

To explain how Christ indwells us and how He makes His home in our hearts, I like to use a glove as an illustration. The glove is made altogether according to the form of the hand so that the hand may get into the glove. Man may be likened to the glove and Christ to the hand. One day when you are saved by believing in Him, Christ enters into you. We have said that when God created us, He created us according to the image of Christ that we may contain Christ. The glove was made according to the form of the hand with one thumb and four fingers; however, the glove is empty because the hand has not yet entered into it. This was our condition before we believed in Jesus. Even after I had believed in Jesus several years, I still did not know that Jesus had come into me like the hand entering into the glove. At that time I read Romans 9:21 again and again, but I simply could not understand. I did not know what the clay, the vessels of honor, and the vessels of dishonor refer to. It was not until one day when I was enlightened to receive the revelation that I fully understood this verse. I saw clearly how the Triune God—the Father, the Son, and the Spirit—was incarnated to become a man, died for me on the cross, and was buried. I also saw how He was resurrected to become the life-giving Spirit and how He has entered into my spirit to be the treasure in me. Furthermore, not only did I understand this matter, but I also found out that this is the central point of the entire New Testament.

CHRIST MAKING HIS HOME
IN OUR MIND, EMOTION, AND WILL

Christ has entered into us and is dwelling in us, but now He still wants to make His home in our hearts. In order to understand this matter, I spent much time studying the New Testament, hoping to find out from the Bible what it means for Christ to make His home in our hearts and how He does it. It has been thirty-three years since 1950, when I began to speak about the mingling of God with man and the indwelling of Christ. I was studying, and during that time I was speaking. Today although I dare not say that I have studied this matter thoroughly, I can say that for the most part I have studied it clearly. Now I will use simple words to tell you how Christ is making His home in our hearts.

First, we need to know that man was created according to the image of Christ. To put it in a simple way, Christ is the expression of God, and He is the very God Himself. The biblical record shows that Christ is full of wisdom; it also shows us His mind. Paul said to the believers in the church in Philippi, "Let this mind be in you, which was also in Christ Jesus" (Phil. 2:5). Furthermore, the Bible shows us the meekness of Christ. In 2 Corinthians 10:1 Paul said, "I myself...entreat you through the meekness...of Christ." The term *meekness* has many denotations. It refers to an expression and a virtue. To be meek is to be mild toward men, without resisting or disputing. This virtue comes out of our nature and our character. Nature is something inherent, whereas character is something expressed. Our nature and character are related to our mind, emotion, and will. Therefore, in order to be meek, we must have meekness inwardly as our nature and then we must manifest it outwardly as our character. This nature must be something produced out of our mind, emotion, and will. It is not something dead. You cannot say that a piece of wood or a table is meek. You can say, for example, that they are smooth. Smoothness is not something of our nature or our character, because it does not require the functions of our mind, emotion, and will. Meekness not only comes out of our mind, emotion, and will, but it also comes out of our conscience and spirit. It comes out of what you are, that is, your inner person;

it also comes out of what you do, that is, your personality manifested outwardly.

Meekness is the image of the Lord Jesus, which is what He is and what He does. The four Gospels in the New Testament show us that the Lord was a meek person. Hence, meekness is a photo of Jesus Christ. His entire human life, His thirty-three and a half years of living on earth, was full of meekness. His mind was a mind of meekness, His emotion was an emotion of meekness, and His will was a will of meekness. His character was meek, His heart was meek, and His Spirit was meek. His soul, His heart, and His Spirit were meek. His entire being was full of meekness. This was the image of the Lord Jesus.

Now let us look at ourselves. God created us as proper human beings according to Christ. We know that all the things were created by God according to their kind. Birds are according to the bird-kind, fish are according to the fish-kind, dogs are according to the dog-kind, cats are according to the cat-kind, walnuts are according to the walnut-kind, and apples are according to the apple-kind. Then, man is according to which kind? Man is according to God's kind because man was created according to the image of God, which is Christ. Hence, man was created according to the image of Christ for the purpose of containing Christ. After we have believed in Christ, He comes in to dwell in us and to make His home in our hearts. However, according to our experience, Christ's making His home in our hearts requires a long period of time and process.

A person may have already believed in the Lord for quite a period of time and Christ has been in him in quite a deep way. However, Christ is like the hand that has entered into the glove but has not been able to extend the fingers into the proper places. Hence, such a one still needs a period of time to enjoy Christ continually and have the fellowship of life with the brothers and sisters. Only after Christ has gained and occupied more ground in him can He begin to make His home in this one. This is just like placing the thumb of the hand into the thumb of the glove. This is also similar to moving into a new house; when the owner puts a large piece of furniture in a suitable place in the new bedroom, he begins the process of his making home in the new house. Then the one that Christ is making His home in continues to attend meetings and have fellowship with the brothers and sisters, call on the name of the Lord, and enjoy the Lord by eating and drinking Him. Gradually another "finger" goes in and Christ thus makes His home in another room. After another period of time, another "finger" goes in and Christ thus makes His home in still another room.

In this way Christ is making His home in our hearts little by little. This process of making home in us is very slow, and it may not be fully accomplished even after we have passed through all the days of our entire life. The higher the life is, the slower is the process of growth. The life within us is indeed very high, so its growth is exceedingly slow. Only lower forms of life can grow speedily. Hence, you should not expect to grow quickly, because the life in you is the highest life. Although Christ as our life grows very slowly, He is growing in us steadily and solidly.

Ephesians 3:17 does not say that "Christ may make His home in you." Instead, it explicitly says that "Christ may make His home in your hearts." Our heart is composed of all the parts of our soul—mind, emotion, and will—plus our conscience, the main part of our spirit. Our heart is joined to our soul and is also connected with our spirit. The real center of our being is not in our outward body but in our inward heart. Our heart—which is joined to the soul, connected with the spirit, and composed of the mind, the emotion, the will, and the conscience—is the totality of all our inward parts. When Christ makes His home in our heart, He controls our entire inward being, and He also supplies and strengthens every inward part with Himself. This is not just an illustration; it is a fact.

Christ not only enters into us, but He also wants to make His home in our heart. When Christ comes into us, He comes into our spirit. Yet it is very likely that He merely stays there and has not entered into the different parts of our heart. Hence, He is waiting within us for us to love Him and cooperate with Him, and He is also waiting for us to know Him and take Him as life. If we love Him and cooperate with Him, we afford Him the opportunity to come into our mind to become its content. This is just like the thumb of our hand getting into the thumb of a glove to be its content. You have believed in the Lord, yet your mind may be void of Christ. Instead, your mind may be filled with your children and spouse and your property. In your mind there is no Christ; rather, there are just yourself and things that are outside of Christ. You have shut Christ outside the door of your mind. Therefore, although He is in your spirit, He is suffering because He cannot get into your mind. This is the real situation of many among us.

TAKING THE MIND OF CHRIST
AS OUR MIND TO BEGIN LIVING CHRIST

If you love the Lord, you should say, "O Lord, I want to take Your mind as my mind. Now I am thinking about my spouse, my children, my studies, and my work. Lord, I don't want to consider them according to my mind. I want You to come into my mind to be its contents so that I may think according to Your mind." This is to live Christ. To begin living Christ is to let the mind of Christ be your mind and consider everything that is related to you, including any person, matter, and thing, according to the mind of Christ. In this way Christ can enter and occupy your mind, and you can take His mind as your mind.

ALLOWING CHRIST TO ENTER
INTO OUR EMOTION AND WILL

Furthermore, Christ will gradually enter into your emotion and will. Before Christ enters into your emotion, whatever you love, you love according to your own preference and not according to Christ's preference. In your love, in your emotion, there is no Christ. Likewise, in your will there is also no Christ. You decide whatever you want, and whatever you say counts; you are the directing one. You make proposals, but in your proposals there is no Christ. Yet when Christ enters into you, His intention is not merely to be in you but to make His home in your heart. His desire is to gradually take over and saturate every part of your heart. Our experience tells us that when we are filled with Him, He is real and living and can freely make His home in our mind, emotion, and will. At this stage, He is everywhere in our being. He is in our spirit, and He is also in our soul. Thus, He occupies and saturates our entire being. Now His indwelling us is His making His home in our heart. As a result, we do not live by ourselves but by Him, and we do not live out ourselves but Christ.

This is to take Christ as our life. In this way we are completely and practically joined to Him as one, and it is at this stage that we are truly Christ-men. A real Christ-man is one who not only has Christ in him but one who is also filled and saturated with Christ and through whom Christ is expressed. This is called Christ's indwelling.

CHAPTER FIVE

HOW TO EXPERIENCE CHRIST'S INDWELLING

Scripture Reading: Phil. 1:19-21; 2:3-8; 3:6b-9; 4:8-9, 13

We have covered the indwelling Christ and Christ's indwelling in the previous chapters. Now let us see how we can experience Christ's indwelling. The entire Bible tells us a wonderful and mysterious thing, that is, that the Triune God desires to work Himself into His believers. He wants to abide in them to be their life. This is the revelation in the Bible. We have said that the mystery of the universe is God; God is the answer to all the mysteries of the universe. How wonderful it is that this God, who is the mystery of the universe, has entered into us to be our life.

Genesis chapter one says that God created the heavens, the earth, and all things. Chapter two says that God formed man of the dust of the ground. God created the heavens, the sun, the rain, and the air for the earth. The earth brought forth herbs and grains for man's existence. God created man after He had finished His creation of the heavens, the earth, and all things.

MAN BEARING GOD'S IMAGE

In Genesis 1 we are told that God created all things according to their kind: fish according to the fish-kind and birds according to the bird-kind. Every living thing was according to its kind and belongs to its kind. But God created man in His image and according to His likeness (vv. 26-27). Therefore, man is according to God's kind. Since man was created in God's image, man's image is God's image; man is a photograph of God. For example, if you want your relatives to see me, but you are unable to bring me to them, then you can take a picture of me and bring it with you. Although this picture is not the real me, it can somewhat show them my outward appearance because it is my picture. The Bible tells us that man was created in God's image. Man is just like a photograph taken according to the likeness of God.

On the one hand, the Bible says that God created man in His image, but on the other hand, it says that God is invisible. Furthermore, Colossians 1:15 says that Christ is the image of the invisible God. God is invisible, yet He has an image; this is truly wonderful. The image mentioned in the Bible does not refer to the outward appearance, which is visible, but rather to the inward nature, which is invisible. For example, we often say that a son looks like his father. If the father is round-faced, the son is also round-faced; if the father has big eyes and large ears, then the son also has big eyes and large ears. This is an outward resemblance. Another kind of resemblance is a resemblance in nature. If the father is meek and kind, so also is the son; if the father is soft-spoken, so also is the son. God created man in His image; this image refers not to the outward appearance but to the inward nature.

GOD'S IMAGE BEING
LOVE, LIGHT, HOLINESS, AND RIGHTEOUSNESS

Colossians 2:9 says, "For in Him [Christ] dwells all the fullness of the Godhead bodily." According to the revelation in the Bible, the essential nature of the Godhead is first, love; second, it is light; third, it is holiness; and fourth, it is righteousness. God is kind and God is full of brightness, because God is love and God is light. Love and light do not have an image; they are divine attributes and characteristics. Love, light, holiness, and righteousness are the essential nature of the Godhead. God is God because He is love, light, holiness, and righteousness. Love and holiness are the nature of God's essence; light and righteousness are the nature of God's expression. In Himself, God is love and holiness. When He is expressed, He is light and righteousness. Furthermore, God is a thoughtful God, and He is also rich in emotions. He loves, and He also shows anger. He has feelings of joy, anger, sorrow, and delight. The Bible also tells us that God is a God of purpose and action; therefore, He is also a God with a will.

THE CREATED MAN HAVING GOD'S IMAGE

Now let us look at man. Man also has the same three aspects. Man is thoughtful, man has emotions, and man has a will. This means that man has God's image. God is wise and thoughtful, God is rich in emotions, and God has a strong will. When God created man, He created man according to such an image. God has thoughts, so He created us with a mind; God has emotions, so He created man also with emotions; God has a will, so He created man also with a will.

Moreover, the conventional ethics that we profess are included in these four items of what God is—love, light, holiness, and righteousness. If your daily walk is full of love, light, holiness, and righteousness, then you are a perfect man. The conventional ethics defined by men are implied in these four items. We were created according to such an image of God. God wants us to be loving and kind; He wants us to be honest and upright; He wants us to be holy and uncontaminated; He wants us to be righteous, not practicing unrighteousness. Throughout the ages, in all lands, among all peoples, whether barbaric or civilized, anyone who steals will have a sense of shame and darkness. A person does not have to be educated to develop this sense because it is inherent in his created nature. Children have a desire to honor their parents and to love and care for others because these qualities are inherent in the created human nature.

THE BATTLE BETWEEN GOOD AND EVIL

However, after man fell, the evil element entered into man causing man to have the evil nature. Consequently, man acquired a corrupted nature that was in opposition to the goodness in him from creation. The realization of the good nature of man, which came from creation, and the evil nature of man, which came in after the fall, divided the Chinese philosophers into two schools. One school believed in the innate goodness of man, while the other school believed in his innate evil. It is correct to say that man is innately good;

this refers to God's creation. It is also correct to say that man is innately evil; this refers to man's fall. The goodness in man is God's creation according to His image. Goodness is a part of man's created nature. This goodness includes love, light, holiness, and righteousness. The sum of love, light, holiness, and righteousness is goodness. To love others is good, to be honest and upright is good, to be holy is good, and to be righteous is good. Conversely, to be unkind, dishonest, unholy, or unrighteous is evil. This evil originates from Satan, the devil.

We have to know assuredly that God created us with an innate goodness. Sometimes we may provoke our parents to anger, but when we calm down, we have a genuine sense that we have wronged them. This is what the Chinese refer to as the awakening of one's conscience. As another example, a husband may have an exchange of words with the wife in the morning, but by the evening he feels sorry for his behavior. This is also the working of the conscience. We know that man is constituted of three layers: the outermost layer is the body, the innermost layer is the spirit, and the middle layer is the soul. Within the three-layered man, the innermost spirit includes intuition, fellowship, and conscience. The conscience is the natural goodness, the "bright virtue" referred to by Confucius.

According to God's creation, man has a life that is good. For example, every time you help someone, you feel happy and glorious. However, if you take advantage of others, for example, by surreptitiously putting their belongings into your pocket, you may think it is profitable, yet within you there is a sense of dishonor and guilt. God created us with an innate goodness. Therefore, do not pay too much attention to the beauty in your appearance. Our appearance is not worth much. As the Chinese say, virtue surpasses beauty. Man was created in God's image; this refers to virtue. This virtue includes a proper mind, a healthy emotion, and a strong will that are manifested through love, light, holiness, and righteousness.

THE LORD JESUS AS THE EXPRESSION OF LOVE, LIGHT, HOLINESS, AND RIGHTEOUSNESS

One day God, the Creator of the universe, became flesh.

He was conceived in the womb of a virgin through the Holy Spirit and was born to be a man, whose name was Jesus. The Bible tells us that all the elements of God were in this man, Jesus. All the fullness of the Godhead dwelt in Jesus Christ bodily (Col. 2:9). At the age of thirty, He came out to preach. All that He was and all that He did, every movement and every action, fully manifested the wisdom of His mind, the richness of His emotions, and the strength of His will. He was exceedingly sober in His mind and very rich in His emotions. In at least two instances in the Bible, it was recorded that He wept (John 11:35; Luke 19:41). Moreover, He had a very resolute will. When He was going to Jerusalem to suffer death, even though many disagreed with Him and advised Him not to go, none was able to stop Him from going. With His face set like a flint, He went boldly to Jerusalem (9:51) and went to the cross to shed His blood and die on our behalf. His will was exceedingly firm. He is God, who possesses thoughts, purpose, and emotions. He lived out a life that was full of love, light, holiness, and righteousness. The life that He lived on the earth was the expression of love, light, holiness, and righteousness.

The four Gospels constitute the biography of the Lord Jesus in four aspects. There are many biographies of renowned men in the world, but there is none that is as inspirational and moving as the biography of the Lord Jesus recorded in the Gospels. Countless people, after reading the four Gospels, have been moved to tears and have even prayed to the Lord. There was a renowned French philosopher who said that if the Lord Jesus in the Gospels was a fabrication, then the fabricator was qualified to be Jesus. This statement is very reasonable. The stories in the Gospels are so marvelous and the words are so mysterious; indeed, they cannot be the speaking of men. The Lord Jesus is not an ordinary historical character; He is God incarnated to be a man, and all that God is dwells in Him. God is thoughtful, and so is the Lord Jesus. God is rich in emotions, and so is the Lord Jesus. God is purposeful with a strong will, and so is the Lord Jesus. God is love, light, holiness, and righteousness. The Lord Jesus is the embodiment of all these four items in all that He was and all that He did, in every word and in every action.

In Philippians, a book on the experience of Christ, Paul said that whatever circumstances he was in, whether through life or through death, Christ would be magnified in his body (1:20). What Paul meant is that in his body Christ's thoughts of wisdom, rich emotions, and steadfast will, as well as Christ's love, light, holiness, and righteousness would be magnified. Regardless of the degree of persecution and regardless of the circumstance, what Paul and the other apostles lived and manifested were thoughts of wisdom, rich emotions, and steadfast will, as well as love, light, holiness, and righteousness. This is the meaning of Christ being magnified in Paul's body.

LIVING CHRIST IN OUR HUMAN VIRTUES

Moreover, in Philippians 1:21 Paul said that to him, to live was Christ. If a person is confused in his mind, muddled in his emotions, and indecisive in his will, he does not have the expression of love, light, holiness, and righteousness, and neither can he live Christ. Furthermore, in 4:8 Paul said, "Brothers, what things are true, what things are dignified, what things are righteous, what things are pure, what things are lovely, what things are well spoken of, if there is any virtue and if any praise, take account of these things." To be true means not to be hypocritical and not to lie. To be dignified means to be worthy of respect and to invite reverence. To be righteous is to be right before God and man. To be pure is to be single in intention and action, without any mixture. To be lovely means to be lovable, agreeable. To be well spoken of means to be of good repute and to be attractive. In addition, there are virtues of excellence and things worthy of praise. These eight items are far superior to the principles of propriety, justice, honesty, and sense of shame taught by the Chinese philosophers. When I was young, I felt it was rather strange that Paul spoke about living Christ in chapters one, two, and three, and then in chapter four, instead of speaking about living Christ, he spoke about living out these virtues.

In 4:9 Paul went on to say, "The things which you have also learned and received and heard and seen in me, practice these things." *These things* refer to the eight items that were previously mentioned. Paul seemed to be saying, "I have lived out these virtues, and you also have to practice these virtues which you have seen in me. In this way the God of peace will be with you. If you live out these virtues, you will enjoy the God of peace."

EXPRESSING THE HUMAN VIRTUES
BY BEING IN CHRIST

Then in 4:13 Paul said, "I am able to do all things in Him who empowers me." *All things* refer to the virtues previously mentioned. When the young people read these eight items, the more they read, the more they will realize that they cannot do these things. They may say, "We have been saved for only a short time, and we are just ordinary people. How can we do these things? Perhaps only the older ones who have been exercised in these things for decades can do them." However, Paul's word here is a promise. He "who empowers me" is Christ, who is also the Spirit of Jesus Christ with a bountiful supply, as mentioned in Philippians 1:19. The Spirit of Jesus Christ is Jesus Christ Himself with a bountiful supply. He supplies and enables us to live out the things that are true, dignified, righteous, pure, lovely, and well spoken of, as well as any virtue and any praise. All we need is just to be in Him, and He will empower us to live out these virtues.

The phrase "in Him who empowers me" does not sound like proper Chinese. Consequently, the translators of the Chinese version of the Bible rendered this verse as "I am able to do all things by Him who empowers me." They rendered *in* as *by,* that is, *by depending upon.* Suppose I cannot walk; then I have to walk by depending upon someone who gives me support. This is the meaning of *by.* But the Bible does not say "by Him" but rather "in Him." This is hard to comprehend. Let me use electricity as an illustration. For example, there are electric lamps, telephones, and other appliances in a house. But if there is no flow of electricity, then the lamps will not light up, the telephones will not work, and all other electrical appliances will not operate. When the electricity is transmitted, then the electric lamps, telephones, and appliances will be "in the electricity"; consequently, the lamps will light up, the telephones will work, and the motors of the other appliances will begin to operate. Strictly speaking, the electric lamp lights up not *by* the electricity but *in* the electricity. Christ is like the electricity; He is the One who empowers us just as the electricity empowers the electrical appliances. We are able to do all things in the "electricity," in Christ, who empowers us.

EXPERIENCING CHRIST'S INDWELLING

Now let us see how we can experience Christ's indwelling. The Lord Jesus was thoughtful. He did many things, none of which was foolish. He spoke many words, none of which was unclear. Whenever He spoke, He spoke just the right amount, neither too much nor too little. His emotions were well balanced. He exercised His anger when warranted but with restraint, and His love was also tempered. Furthermore, His will was steadfast. All His expressions were love, light, holiness, and righteousness. He was true, dignified, righteous, pure, lovely, and well spoken of. Furthermore, He was virtuous and praiseworthy. He was the real goodness and the genuine beauty; He was God. In some ways, we are like Him. He has thoughts, and so do we. He has emotions, and so do we. His will is steadfast, and so is ours. Jesus loves, and so do we. Jesus is honest and upright, and so are we. Jesus is holy, and so are we. Jesus is righteous, and so are we. Although there is a difference in degree, we are of the same kind because we were created in His image.

The Lord Jesus is not only wonderful but also mysterious. When you open up your heart and receive Him as your Savior, He comes into you and dwells in you to be your life and everything. How does He come into you? The Bible says that He died for us, was buried, and was resurrected. Now He has become the life-giving Spirit. Today He is the omnipresent Spirit; He is everywhere. Whoever believes into Him and calls upon Him, He will enter into this one to be his life and content. This is the most marvelous thing in the world. The Lord comes into us to dwell in us, and this is what we refer to as His "indwelling." The indwelling Christ is the embodiment of God and the life-giving, omnipresent Spirit. He has a mind, emotion, and will; He is also love, light, holiness, and righteousness. In the beginning we were created in His image, so we also have a mind, emotion, and will, as well as love, light, holiness, and righteousness. However, we were only an empty shell without the content and reality. We were just like the empty glove that was made in the form of a hand. One day, God became flesh as the Lord Jesus. He lived the human life, died, resurrected, and became the life-giving Spirit. The life-giving Spirit is the Lord Jesus with His mind, emotion, and will and the God who is love, light, holiness, and righteousness. The Spirit enters into us like the hand that fits into the glove to become its content and reality. Thus, we are no longer those who are empty, without content. Our created human virtues are no longer merely a shell because Christ is in us as the reality.

EXPERIENCING ONENESS WITH THE LORD

Second Timothy 4:22 says, "The Lord be with your spirit." This Lord is the life-giving Spirit. When we pray and petition before the Lord, the Spirit comes into our spirit and dwells in us forever. Furthermore, He is waiting for us to love Him. He takes possession of us whenever we say, "Lord Jesus, I love You." The more we love Him, the more we are possessed by Him. The last stanza of *Hymns,* #398 says, "O to be like Thee! While I am pleading / Pour out Thy Spirit, fill with Thy love. / Make me a temple meet for Thy dwelling, / Fit for a life which Thou wouldst approve." That we live a life approved by the Lord means that we take the Lord's mind as our mind, take the Lord's emotion as our emotion, and take the Lord's will as our will. We also take the Lord's love, light, holiness, and righteousness as our love, light, holiness, and righteousness. The Lord and we, we and the Lord, are completely one. We are just the same as He is. For to us, to live is Christ.

The ancient sages in China taught that man is innately good. This is correct. What God created originally was good. He created us with the bright virtue, the innate goodness, which needs to be developed. However, without Christ in us, everything is still a shell devoid of reality. We are just like an empty glove. When the hand gets inside the glove, then the glove has content and reality. Furthermore, the glove and the hand become one; they are a perfect match. This illustrates the oneness between God and man. God and man, man and God, are completely satisfied. If man does not have God, neither God nor man is satisfied; this is the root of dissatisfaction in human life. When man has God, both God and man are satisfied; this is the source of true satisfaction in human life.

Hallelujah! Christ wants to become your mind, emotion, and will. He also wants to be your love, light, holiness, and righteousness. Even the more, He wants to be in you that which is true, dignified, righteous, pure, lovely, well spoken of, virtuous, and praiseworthy. Then, Christ can be expressed through your God-created human virtues.

TO LIVE BEING CHRIST

Every one of us possesses the God-created virtues, the inherent human virtues. But it is very difficult to express these virtues by ourselves, and even if we were able to, the expression would be neither complete nor perfect. We need to be filled by Christ. Our virtues should be vessels that are filled with Christ to manifest the very essence of Christ. This is the highest, perfect virtue. This is the righteousness of God which Paul referred to in Philippians 3:9. Formerly, he pursued the righteousness which he worked out by keeping the law; eventually what he pursued was the righteousness of God lived out through Christ in him. Formerly, he wanted the glove, but eventually he wanted the hand. The hand in the glove is the content and reality of the glove. Eventually, the hand and the glove are one, and the glove becomes the expression of the hand. We are the glove, and He, our beloved Lord, is the hand. Our heart is filled with His love, and our life is one with Him. Thus, for us to live is Christ.

Christ lives in us. He is our life, and we are His living; He is our content, and we are His expression. He and we, we and He, exactly match one another. He and we become one. This is the enjoyment of Christ, the living out of Christ. This is the experience of Christ's indwelling.

CHAPTER SIX

LIVING OUT CHRIST IN HUMAN VIRTUES

(1)

Scripture Reading: Phil. 1:8, 19, 21; 2:1-3; 3:6b-10; 4:8-9

LONGING AFTER THE SAINTS
IN THE BOWELS OF CHRIST JESUS

Philippians 1:8 says, "I...in the inward parts of Christ Jesus." In the Chinese Union Version this verse is translated as: "I...understand the bowels of Christ Jesus." This rendering seems to be saying that the bowels of Christ Jesus are His alone and that I just sympathize with and understand His bowels. He is He, and I am I; His bowels are His, and I am sympathetic towards Him. Therefore, I understand His bowels. This kind of rendering separates Christ from us. This, however, is not Paul's notion in the original text. According to the original text, what Paul said was, "I...in the bowels of Christ Jesus." By saying this, he joined himself to Christ Jesus and became one with Him.

Instead of only outwardly understanding the bowels of Christ Jesus, Paul was in the bowels of Christ Jesus. Paul was not only in Christ, but even more he was in the bowels of Christ Jesus. This shows us that we who believe in the Lord Jesus are joined to Him and are one with Him; hence, His bowels are our bowels. Before we were saved, we did not have the bowels of the Lord Jesus; we had only ours. After we are saved, the Lord Jesus enters into our being, and we have His bowels. Hence, we no longer walk or conduct ourselves according to our bowels but according to His bowels.

Every spiritual matter is a story of life, and it is mysterious and incomprehensible. Yet our God frequently uses His created things with their natural phenomena to explain the hidden mysteries. The grafting of trees is a good example. In grafting, a good branch is joined to a poor tree. How can we make a peach tree produce sweet fruit instead of sour fruit? It is by grafting a branch of the good peach tree to the sour peach tree. Originally, these two trees have two distinct and different lives, but after the grafting process, the two become one. The life that produces the sour peaches can no longer grow because the old branch that grows out of the roots of the sour peach tree has been cut off, and the good branch has been grafted in; therefore, new fruit comes out of the good branch. The new fruit, which is the result of the mingling of two lives, is no longer sour and ugly but sweet and beautiful.

When we believe in the Lord Jesus, He as the new branch is grafted into us as the old tree. Therefore, we need to realize that our old man must be terminated and put to death, so that Christ can grow in us and be magnified through us. Every day, by the Spirit, we need to put to death the old practices of the body. We should not give them any opportunity to grow, so that Christ can grow in us daily. Paul said, "I long after you all in the inward parts of Christ Jesus." Paul's longing after the saints was in the Lord, even in the bowels, the inward parts, of the Lord Jesus. Therefore, it was not his longing in himself alone; rather, it was his longing in the Lord, in his union with the Lord.

ENJOYING THE BOUNTIFUL SUPPLY OF THE SPIRIT OF JESUS CHRIST

Philippians 1:19 refers to "the bountiful supply of the Spirit of Jesus Christ." The Spirit of Jesus Christ is Jesus Christ Himself. The Spirit of Jesus Christ has a bountiful supply. The phrase *bountiful supply* has a special meaning in Greek. In ancient Greece there were choruses, and the *choragus,* the leader of the chorus, was responsible for supplying all the needs of the members of the chorus by providing them with instruments, costumes, food, lodging, and other matters. The choragus supplied whatever the chorus needed.

The supply of the choragus was the "bountiful supply" referred to in this verse.

The bountiful supply of the all-inclusive Spirit of Jesus Christ enabled Paul to magnify and live Christ in anguish, in persecution, in peril, in tribulation, and even in imprisonment. Since Paul and the Lord Jesus were completely joined as one, the bowels of the Lord Jesus became the bowels of Paul. Paul lived in the bowels of the Lord Jesus and regarded the Lord's bowels as his own bowels. Hence, the Spirit of Jesus Christ as his bountiful supply enabled him to always magnify Christ, whether in death or in life, in woe or in blessing, in pain or in joy, in sorrow or in delight. Therefore, for him to live was Christ. This is the experience of Paul in Philippians chapter one, and this should be our experience as well.

ENCOURAGEMENT, CONSOLATION, AND FELLOWSHIP IN CHRIST

Philippians 2:1 says, "If there is therefore any encouragement in Christ, if any consolation of love, if any fellowship of spirit, if any tenderheartedness and compassions." Philippians 1 shows us that Paul was one with Christ. Philippians 2 shows us that the believers are also one with Christ. In chapter two Paul began by saying "in Christ." This tells us that all the encouragement, consolation, and fellowship are in Christ. Paul was not speaking about the things outside of Christ. Therefore, Christians must live and walk in Christ. In the phrase *if any fellowship of spirit, spirit* refers not to the Holy Spirit but to the regenerated human spirit. In the phrase *if any tenderheartedness and compassions,* the Greek word for *tenderheartedness* is literally *bowels,* the same word for *inward parts* in 1:8, signifying the tender, inward affections. Therefore, it is appropriately translated as *tenderheartedness.*

BEING FOUND IN CHRIST

Philippians 3 shows us that Paul considered the knowledge of Christ as an excellency; on account of Christ he counted all things, including even the righteousness which was out of the law, to be loss that he might gain Christ.

Formerly, Paul had been zealous for the law to the extent that he persecuted the Christians, but he turned from the law of Moses to Christ. Therefore, when others saw him, they found him to be a man in Christ. He no longer had the righteousness which was out of the law, but he had the righteousness which was through faith in Christ. This righteousness is the righteousness of God, not the righteousness of Paul. Paul could have this righteousness because the resurrected Christ who lived in him caused him to experience the power of the resurrection of Christ.

EXPRESSING GOD IN HUMAN VIRTUES

Philippians 4:8-9 lists six precious virtues: truthfulness, dignity, righteousness, purity, loveliness, and being well spoken of. In addition, there are virtue and praise as the summing up of the six items, which include all the good qualities found in the Chinese ethical teachings.

Truthfulness does not mean to be truthful in matter of fact, without falsehood. Instead, it means to be genuine and trustworthy in conduct, not to play politics, but to be sincere and honest. The term *dignity* is rich in meaning; it refers to being venerable without putting on airs. A person whose conduct is weighty and dignified will invite respect. *Righteousness* means being right, correct, proper, unbiased, and fair. *Purity* refers to being single in intention, motive, and action, without any mixture. Then, anything that is true, dignified, right, or pure is lovely (agreeable) and well spoken of. Finally, Paul summed up these six items with this word: "If there is any virtue and if any praise." In Greek the word for *virtue* means "excellence." It refers to the state of ethical energy exhibited in vigorous action. Such excellent exhibition will naturally elicit praise from people. These eight items are grouped in pairs. "What things are true" and "what things are dignified" form a group; "what things are righteous" and "what things are pure" form another group; "what things are lovely" and "what things are well spoken of" form still another group; and "any virtue" and "any praise" form the last group. These are moral virtues in the Bible. These were the things which people saw and heard in Paul. Paul testified that if we live out such a life, the God of peace will be with us.

MAN AS GOD'S VESSEL TO EXPRESS HIM

The Bible tells us that man is a special creation of God, different from the trees and flowers and from the oxen and sheep. Man is God's unique creation in the universe. Man is unique in that he was created to be a vessel of God. God created man with the purpose of entering into man that He and man might be mingled as one. He wants to be the life in man that man might live Him out. The life of God within man is just God Himself, and the living out of God is the expression of the life within. In other words, God wants man to live Him out. This is the most mysterious truth in the Bible. Unfortunately, not only do the unbelievers not understand this, but even many Christians do not know this truth. Nevertheless, this is the central revelation in the Bible.

Man was created to be God's vessel to contain God and to express God. God wanted to enter into man to be his life, and man was to express God in his living. For this reason, God created man in His image. We mentioned earlier that God is light, love, holiness, and righteousness. Light, love, holiness, and righteousness comprise the aforementioned virtues: truthfulness, dignity, righteousness, purity, loveliness, and being well spoken of. Moreover, God has His thoughts, emotions, and will; He is also purposeful. God's image refers to all these attributes and virtues, and it is according to such an image that God created man. Although man often commits sins and does evil due to the fall, there is still a desire in him to attain to a higher plane, a desire to be honorable, kind, holy, and righteous.

The Ten Commandments which God decreed through Moses are a portrait of the nature of God. The first commandment is to have no other gods. The second commandment is to not make graven images nor to worship and serve idols. The third commandment is to not take the name of Jehovah God in vain, that is, to not use His name in vain in things other than God Himself. The fourth commandment is to remember the Sabbath day. The Sabbath denotes that man becomes one with God to enjoy all that He has accomplished. To keep the Sabbath is to acknowledge and enjoy what God has accomplished for man. In six days God created the heavens, the earth, and all the things therein, and lastly He created man. Then on the seventh day He rested from His work. Therefore, immediately after man was created, he began to enjoy the rest established by God; that is, he began to enjoy all of God's creation. These are the first four commandments of the Ten Commandments. God's desire is that man be one with Him. Besides God, man should have no other gods. He should not make any graven images, and he should not bow down or serve idols. He should not take the name of God in vain, that is, not vainly use the name of God in things other than God. Moreover, man should remember the Sabbath and be one with God to enjoy all that God has accomplished for man. This is on God's side.

The last six of the Ten Commandments, which are on man's side, include the following: honor your parents, do not murder, do not commit adultery, do not steal, do not testify with false testimony against your neighbors, and do not covet. The last commandment touches our inner heart most deeply. Some people may be able to fulfill the first nine commandments, but the last one is the most difficult to fulfill. In Philippians 3:6 Paul said that he was blameless according to the righteousness of the law. However, in Romans 7 he confessed that he was not able to overcome covetousness (v. 8). Paul showed us that ultimately man is unable to fulfill the law. Moreover, he showed us that even if he had the ability to fulfill the first nine commandments, he would give it all up because the righteousness of the law had replaced Christ. Anyone who seeks after the righteousness of the law and rejects Christ, who is the reality of the law, is just like one who cares only for the glove and rejects the hand, so that eventually the glove replaces the hand. The righteousness of the law must not replace Christ.

CHRIST AS THE REALITY OF ALL HUMAN VIRTUES

Man was created in God's image, possessing the image of God's virtues. Christ is the embodiment of God, the reality of God's virtues. When you receive Christ into you, your love becomes one of His "rooms," your righteousness becomes another "room," and your holiness becomes still another "room." All your human virtues become His habitation. Do not think that because we are those who live in Christ, we do not practice ethics and morality. No! Our ethics and morality are higher and more real because they are not our own work but the living out of Christ in our human virtues.

Formerly, when we did not have Christ, we conducted ourselves with all propriety, observed the moral principles, and upheld the ceremonies for courtesy. However, like an empty glove, everything we did was without the real content. It is only after we have received Christ that He becomes our life, reality, and content. When man was created, he had the human virtues in him, but all these virtues were devoid of reality, because only Christ is the reality of all these virtues. When Christ comes into our being, He makes every virtue real. Thus, our love towards others becomes real, and our honoring of our parents becomes real. This is because these virtues are the living out of Christ from within us.

LIVING OUT CHRIST IN HUMAN VIRTUES

According to the revelation in the Bible, God went through four steps to enable man to live out Christ in human virtues. First, God created all things in the universe and in particular He created man in His image. Second, He decreed the law. The content of the law is a portrait of God's image. God is light, so the law also gives light; God is compassionate, so the law also shows compassion; God is holy and righteous, so the law is also holy and righteous. Man was created in God's image; likewise, the law was also written according to God's image. Accordingly, the law and man should be in complete harmony. But man fell and was not able to live and walk according to what was written in the law. In other words, fallen man cannot express God.

Third, God was incarnated and became the man Jesus, who lived on earth for thirty-three and a half years. What the Lord Jesus lived out on earth was exactly what was portrayed in the law. In the four Gospels, we see that the human living of Jesus was just the expression of God. He was love, light, holiness, and righteousness; He was also full of thoughts, emotions, and intentions. The Lord Jesus lived out God exactly according to what God is.

Now we see that man was created in God's image, that the law was written according to what God is, and that the Lord Jesus lived out a life that was according to what God is. Concerning these three steps, some Christians have a misconception. They think that since the Lord Jesus lived out the likeness of God, He is qualified to be our pattern and we should imitate Him. In fact, however, Christians who try to imitate Jesus are just like monkeys trained to imitate men eating food with a fork; that is a mere performance and not the genuine living. Therefore, man cannot live Christ by imitating Him. Hence, man needs the fourth step of God's work. In this step, after the Lord Jesus lived out God for men to see, He went to die for them and shed His blood for the redemption of their sins, and then He was resurrected to become the life-giving Spirit. When we receive this pneumatic Christ, He enters into us to be our life and lives out the image of God from within us. This is the way for Christians to live out Christ.

Since the Lord Jesus lives in us, He uplifts our love toward others, causing us to love them in a more real and sincere way. We no longer love by ourselves, but we love by the Christ who lives within us. It is not we who love, but it is Christ who loves in us. Paul said, "I am crucified with Christ; and it is no longer I who live, but it is Christ who lives in me" (Gal. 2:20). It is Christ who is lived out in our human virtues. In this way children will surely honor their parents, husbands will surely love their wives, and wives will surely submit to their husbands. You will conduct yourself in a way that is upright, true, dignified, righteous, pure, lovely, and well spoken of. Your living and your every move will be excellent and worthy of praise. Nevertheless, all these are not by your own effort; rather, it is Christ who lives in your spirit and who lives out of you.

Today Christ is the Spirit. Not only can He be in us, but we also can be in Him. This is just like the air. The air can get into us, and we can also be in the air. The Lord is like the air; on the one hand, He is in us, and on the other hand, we are in Him. We are mingled with Him as one. His life and our life have become one. This is not an exchanged life but a grafted life. Therefore, we no longer live by our natural life, but we live through Him and by Him. Consequently, He is lived out in our human virtues.

The Christ who lives in us is the Spirit with a bountiful supply and the One who empowers us. He has become one with us. Therefore, we do not have to depend on our own strength to keep the law and work out the righteousness which is out of the law. We have to reject ourselves, take Christ as life, and live by Him. Then He will be the bountiful supply in our spirit. If we allow Him to live out through us, then what is lived out is not our own righteousness but the righteousness of Christ. The righteousness which we have by keeping the law is the expression of ourselves. But if because of our faith in Christ we reject ourselves and allow Christ to live out from us, then what we express is not our own righteousness by our own keeping of the law but the righteousness which is out of God through faith in Him. This righteousness is the expression of God and the magnification of Christ. This is to live Christ. When Christ is lived out from us, He is lived out from our human virtues.

CHAPTER SEVEN

LIVING OUT CHRIST IN HUMAN VIRTUES

(2)

Scripture Reading: Phil. 1:8, 19-21; 2:1-5, 3:6b-10; 4:8-9, 13

TWO ASPECTS IN THE BOOK OF PHILIPPIANS

I believe that after reading the above verses from the book of Philippians, we can sense that the words are so sweet and precious. These precious words involve two aspects; the first aspect concerns us and the second aspect concerns the Lord. Concerning our side, the human side, Paul refers to the matter of "bowels." He says that if there is any encouragement in Christ, if any consolation of love, if any fellowship of spirit, if any tenderheartedness (literally, bowels) and compassions, we should think the same thing, have the same love, being joined in soul, and think the one thing. Furthermore, on the negative side, Paul tells us that we should not do anything out of selfish ambition or vainglory, but that in lowliness of mind each one should consider others more excellent than himself. Then in 4:8, Paul gives us six virtues with two additional items as a summation. These six virtues are truthfulness, dignity, righteousness, purity, loveliness, and being well spoken of. The two items of summation are virtue and praise. Paul wants us to consider these things.

The book of Philippians also presents the aspect concerning the Lord. The aspect concerning us is easy to comprehend. However, the aspect concerning the Lord is too extraordinary and therefore is more difficult to comprehend. Philippians 1:19 says, "Through...the bountiful supply of the Spirit of Jesus Christ"; 3:10 says, "To know...the power of His resurrection";

4:13 says, "In Him who empowers me"; lastly, 4:9 says, "The God of peace." These words are not easy to comprehend because they are transcendent and uncommon. However, in the verses of our Scripture reading, some of the wordings show us that the two aspects are connected. For example, in the phrase *the bowels of Christ Jesus, Christ Jesus* involves the Lord, who is transcendent, while *bowels* involves us, who are human. These two aspects become one in Christ. Another example, the verse concerning taking the mind of Jesus Christ as our mind (2:5), also joins Christ Jesus and us together.

Many people in Christianity preach from the book of Philippians, especially concerning the human aspect. We can hear this kind of preaching in almost all Christian congregations. However, few speak about the transcendent aspect of the Lord. Among us, however, we always speak about the transcendent aspect of the Lord. We constantly preach concerning the bountiful supply of the Spirit of Jesus Christ, the power of the resurrection of Christ, Christ as the One who empowers us, and the enjoyment of the God of peace. When I was young, I heard much preaching on the book of Philippians in relation to man, but after I became older, I began to preach concerning the transcendent aspect of the Lord.

However, the Lord has shown me in recent years that it is not right to speak only about the transcendent aspect of the Lord and put the human aspect behind. I did what I did because I received a negative impression from Christianity when I was young. Because most Christians are not clear about the truths concerning the human aspect in the book of Philippians, when they hear someone speaking about human virtues, such as tenderheartedness, kindness, compassion, humility, being without vainglory, truthfulness, dignity, righteousness, purity, loveliness, and being well spoken of, they question in their heart, "Aren't these the same as the teachings of Confucius, Mencius, and other philosophers?" Therefore, since I came to America, I have been speaking specifically concerning the transcendent aspect of the Lord. For this reason some people misunderstood me and thought that I speak only about the Spirit and not about ethics. In fact, the Christian virtues referred to in the Bible are far superior to the ethics taught by Confucius and Mencius. The believers' virtues taught in the Bible are lived out by Christ from within the believers. We Christians are precious in that we have God in us, we have the Spirit of Jesus Christ as our bountiful supply, we have the resurrection power of Christ operating in us, and we have Christ empowering us. Such a God in us becomes our peace and our daily enjoyment. Therefore, we spontaneously live out the surpassing human virtues.

LIVING OUT CHRIST IN HUMAN VIRTUES

I have already spoken a number of times on the book of Philippians. During the 1980 Summer Training on the Life-study of Philippians, I gave thirty messages; soon thereafter I gave another series of more than thirty messages. Those messages were combined into a printed volume of sixty-two messages. However, in all those messages I did not point out this particular subject—living out Christ in human virtues. I feel that it is a great advancement to point out this subject. Philippians 1:21 says, "For to me, to live is Christ." This statement should not be considered alone. To understand this statement, we have to understand the entire book of Philippians because this statement is a summary of the entire book. We want to see from this statement what it means to "live out Christ in human virtues."

GOD'S IMAGE—
LOVE, LIGHT, HOLINESS, AND RIGHTEOUSNESS

In the Bible the image of God refers to what God is. God is love, light, holiness, and righteousness. Therefore, love, light, holiness, and righteousness are what God is, hence, His image. Ephesians 4:23 and Colossians 3:10 clearly say that we need to be transformed and renewed into the image of the Lord. God's image is love, light, holiness, and righteousness in reality.

The virtues spoken of in the Bible are summed up in the things that are true, dignified, righteous, pure, lovely, and well spoken of, as well as in virtue and praise, as listed in Philippians 4:8. If we put all these items together and carefully analyze them, we will clearly see that these virtues are love, light, holiness, and righteousness. These four words represent all the virtues in the Bible, which are the expressions of God. God's expression is God's image, which is love, light, holiness, and righteousness.

Human Virtues as
a Photograph of God's Image

Human virtues are a picture of God's image. Many things in the universe are symbols. Suppose you take a picture of me. You may say that the person in the picture is I, yet it is not I. You may also say that it is not I, yet it is I. If you send this picture to someone, saying, "This is Mr. Lee," that is not exactly correct. This is because the person in the picture is actually not I, but only my picture. The picture of a person is not the reality of the person or the person himself; it is merely the image of a person.

Consider yourself. Before you were saved, you desired to be kind, honest, upright, and fair. These desires are innate; they are not the result of any outward teachings. Why was man created this way? It is because man was created in God's image. The first man was a photograph of God. We are all reprints of this photograph. The negative of this photograph can be developed into millions of copies. The descendants of Adam are all reprints of this picture. We are pictures of God, reprints of God. Our relationship with God is so intimate. God is our source, and we are His pictures. God is love, light, holiness, and righteousness; we also have the essence of love, light, holiness, and righteousness.

The Law as
a Portrait of God's Image

We have said earlier that the Ten Commandments given by God through Moses are a portrait of God's nature; therefore, the law is a portrait of God's image. The Ten Commandments may be likened to the menu in a restaurant. You do not go to a restaurant to eat the menu. A menu merely indicates the dishes to be served. The law is merely a "menu" that portrays what God is. Therefore, the contents of the law exactly correspond to the image of God. What the law speaks about are love, light, holiness, and righteousness.

Christ as the Living Out
of God's Image

The law is only a portrait of God's image. It was not until Christ came that the true image of God was expressed. The four Gospels in the New Testament are biographies of the Lord Jesus as the records of His life on the earth. To sum up, the Lord's entire life was the expression of love, light, holiness, and righteousness. He was not merely a portrait or picture of God's image; rather, He was actually a man who lived out God Himself.

Christians as Reprints of Christ

Human virtues are pictures, reprints, of God's image. We who have the life of Christ in us are reprints of Christ. We can see this in Paul's experiences. In Philippians 3:6-8 Paul said, "As to the righteousness which is in the law, become blameless. But what things were gains to me [including the righteousness of the law], these I have counted as loss on account of Christ...on account of the excellency of the knowledge of Christ Jesus my Lord." Paul did not speak of the excellency of Christ Jesus, but of the excellency of the knowledge of Christ Jesus. Formerly he knew only the law and regarded only the keeping of the law as precious, but now he knew Christ and considered his knowledge of Christ as something excellent. Paul's insight had dramatically changed. Now he regarded the righteousness of the law as refuse. Before Paul was saved, he treasured the righteousness which he gained in the law. Consequently, he said that according to the righteousness of the law he was blameless. Now his attitude had completely changed. He said that he considered the righteousness of the law as refuse and therefore forsook it in order to gain Christ as his life and everything. He wanted Christ, instead of the righteousness of the law, to be his righteousness.

Righteousness here may also be explained as virtues. Paul

did not have virtues on account of the law. Instead, he took Christ as his virtues. Therefore, in verse 9 he went on to say, "And be found in Him, not having my own righteousness which is out of the law, but that which is through faith in Christ, the righteousness which is out of God and based on faith." How could others see that Paul was in Christ? It was because Paul lived Christ. He did not have the righteousness (virtue) which was out of the law but that which was through faith in Christ, the righteousness (virtue) which was out of God. Paul lived Christ and magnified Christ; hence, he became a reprint of Christ.

Through faith in Christ we have been joined to Christ, and another kind of righteousness is manifested through us. This righteousness, which is out of God and based on faith, is just Christ Himself. First Corinthians 1:30 says that Christ became righteousness to us from God. This righteousness is not our morality, our behavior, or the result of our keeping the law. Instead, it is the issue of our being joined to Christ through faith and of Christ's being one with us and living Himself out through us. When others see that Christ is lived out of us, they know that we are in Christ. Thus, we know Christ and the power of His resurrection. We personally experience that Christ in us is living, resurrected, and powerful. He is lived out of us as God's righteousness and expressed through us as our virtues. Whoever lives Christ and expresses Christ in this way is a reprint of Christ.

Able to Do All Things in Christ

In chapter four Paul went on and exhorted us to experience Christ in this way. When we experience Christ, we live out the things that are true, dignified, righteous, pure, lovely, and well spoken of, all of which possess some virtue and something worthy of praise. We can attain to this level because the resurrected Christ is in us empowering us with the power of resurrection. Therefore, Paul said, "I am able to do all things in Him who empowers me" (v. 13). Paul was able to do all things in the One who empowered him. Being able to do all things does not mean being able to earn a Ph.D. or being promoted to general manager just like some others. *All things* refer to the things that are true, dignified, righteous, pure, lovely, and well spoken of, all of which possess some virtue and something worthy of praise, as mentioned in verse 8. Others were not able to do these things, but Paul was able because he was empowered with the power of resurrection through the operation of the resurrected Christ in him.

THE HIGHEST ETHIC—
CHRIST EXPRESSED IN HUMAN VIRTUES

Based on the foregoing speaking, we can derive a conclusion. Philippians is a book on living out Christ in human virtues, such as being true, being dignified, being righteous, being pure, being lovely, and being well spoken of. Christ is our virtues. When Christ is lived out through us, we are actually living out Christ. Because Christ is the expression of God, when Christ is lived out through us, divinity is expressed through humanity. Thus, God's original purpose in the creation of man is attained, and what is portrayed in the law is also more than adequately fulfilled and realized.

To live out Christ in man's virtues is to live out Christ in the virtues which God created in man. We do not disregard ethics, but we disregard ethics that are devoid of Christ. We want virtues that are filled with Christ. Here lies the superiority of biblical ethics, which are human virtues expressed through God as life in man. Biblical ethics are the virtues lived out from us by the Christ who has entered into us after He was incarnated, lived on the earth for thirty-three and a half years, passed through death and resurrection, became the life-giving Spirit, and ascended to the throne. As the Christ who died and resurrected and as the all-inclusive Spirit, He lives in us as our life to express His image through us. The expression of His image is the highest human virtue.

No other ethic in the world is higher than this kind of virtue. All virtues expressed in human conduct, religious philosophy, human ethics, laws, and rituals cannot compare with this. Today, what the overcoming and sanctified Christians live out is Christ. The perfect conduct that is expressed through them is the highest virtue.

We should be truthful, dignified, righteous, pure, lovely,

and well spoken of; we should have all kinds of virtues and receive all kinds of praises. However, these characteristics must not be devoid of content. The content is not we, but Christ. Our truthfulness is Christ; our loveliness is Christ; our dignity is Christ; our righteousness is Christ; our purity is Christ; our being well spoken of is Christ; any virtue and any praise we have are Christ, who is the image of God. Today when we live Christ, we live out the image of God in our human virtues for the glory of God. Consequently, God becomes our enjoyment and satisfaction. Hence, He is also our God of peace. The *God of peace* means that God is the One whom we can enjoy and the One who can satisfy us. The apostle Paul lived out this kind of life, and he also hoped that every Christian also will live this kind of life.

CHAPTER EIGHT

THE SUBJECTIVE SALVATION
OF THE TRIUNE GOD

Scripture Reading: Phil. 1:19-21; 3:10a; 4:13; 2:12b-13; 4:6-9

EXPERIENCING THE TRIUNE GOD AS OUR LIFE AND EXPRESSING HIM IN OUR HUMAN VIRTUES

In the previous chapters we saw how to experience Christ as our life and how to live out Christ in our human virtues. In general, Christians consider human virtues as the so-called ethics. However, from the Word of God we have seen that we are not speaking about ethics. Rather, we are speaking about Christ as our life being lived out of us, that is, Christ being lived out in our human virtues and becoming the expression of our perfect living. Therefore, we should not confuse Christian good behavior with man's ethics. Christian virtues are altogether different from the conventional ethics taught by the Chinese people.

The book of Philippians is a book on experiencing Christ. This book speaks about how to magnify Christ in our body. In 1:20 Paul said, "In nothing I will be put to shame, but with all boldness, as always, even now Christ will be magnified in my body, whether through life or through death." Paul's desire was that Christ, in whom he believed, after whom he followed, on whom he depended, and in whom he lived, would not only be expressed but also be magnified in his body. Eventually, he could say, "For to me, to live is Christ" (v. 21a). The perfect living of Paul was the expression of Christ; therefore, for him, to live was Christ. However, do not for a moment think that we have deified Paul. Paul was not God, but he was able to express God. We do not deify ourselves; rather, we have Christ as our life, and He is lived out and magnified through us.

For the past few decades, I preached about the truth concerning living Christ, but because I was still greatly influenced by my traditional background, I did not have the boldness to connect the matter of living out Christ as our life with the matter of our human virtues. However, for the past few years, after I had thoroughly studied the book of Philippians, I realized that, on the one hand, this book speaks about the Triune God as our life operating within us to be our everything, and on the other hand, it speaks about human virtues. From chapter four verse 8, we see that which is true, dignified, righteous, pure, lovely, and well spoken of, as well as any virtue and any praise, all constitute our human virtues. However, these virtues are not the result of our own work but the issue of our experience of the Triune God as our life. Thus, the book of Philippians covers two aspects: One aspect is that the Triune God is our life and is lived out through us; the other aspect is that the good behavior that is lived out from us is our virtues.

GOD'S BEING—
LOVE, LIGHT, HOLINESS, AND RIGHTEOUSNESS

We have said that our God is the Creator of the universe and all things. He was incarnated to be a man, the Lord Jesus, who died and shed His blood for us to be our Redeemer and was resurrected to become the pneumatic Christ to be our life. Such a God is love and light, and He is also holy and righteous. God is love, and this love is transcendent and powerful. He can love the unlovable; He can love beyond what man can love. Not only is He the Giver of love but His very nature is love. God's nature consists of both love and light. Love is inward, and light is outward; love is hidden, and light is expressed. When God's nature is hidden, it is love; when it is expressed, it is light.

The Bible also says that God is holy and righteous. God is not only holy, but He is holiness itself. God is not only righteous, but He is righteousness itself. Holiness is His inward nature, whereas righteousness is His outward expression. Holiness and love belong to the same category; both are the inward nature of God. Righteousness and light belong to the same category; both are the expression of God's nature. God is holiness; this is in relation to Himself. God is light; this is in relation to man. Love expressed is light; holiness expressed is righteousness. These attributes are what God is. Our God is love, light, holiness, and righteousness. Thus, love, light, holiness, and righteousness constitute God's being, God's image.

MAN BEING A PICTURE OF WHAT GOD IS

Genesis 1:26 clearly tells us that God created man in His image. Here, the word *image* refers to what God is. That God created man in His image means that He created man according to what He is. He is love, light, holiness, and righteousness. Therefore, the man that He created had the image of love, light, holiness, and righteousness.

Upon hearing these words and after examining yourself, you may say, "I do not have love. I strike and scold people; how can I love? Furthermore, I am not in the light; rather, I have done many things in darkness. Moreover, I am not holy; rather, I am impure, my heart is unclean, and my whole being is filthy. And I am not righteous; my conduct is improper, and I like to take advantage of others." Your assessment of yourself is correct in that your conduct is altogether the conduct of a fallen man. However, in the silence of the night, when you examine yourself, you will sense that in the innermost part of your being there are love, light, holiness, and righteousness. You hate to be corrupt; rather, you like to be pure, holy, and noble. You do not like to do evil, to cheat, or to act craftily; rather, you desire your conduct to be upright and full of righteousness. This is reflected in the theory of "men being born naturally good." According to man's created nature, this is correct. Indeed, within man there is the God-created goodness.

God created man in His image. Just as God is love, so there is also love in man. Therefore, man does not like to strike or scold people. Just as God is light, so there is also light in man. Therefore, man does not like to do the things of darkness. Just as God is holiness, so there is also holiness in man. Therefore, man does not delight in being corrupt. Just as God is righteousness, so there is also righteousness in man. Therefore, man likes to be just and fair. The love, light, holiness, and righteousness in man are all created according to what God is. Therefore, human virtues are a picture of God's image. However, although a picture shows the appearance of the object, it is not the real object itself. In the beginning, man was created perfect, having the image of love and light but without the reality. Man was only an empty shell. God had not yet entered into him to be his content and reality.

THE EXPOSING LAW AS
A PORTRAIT OF WHAT GOD IS

God's original purpose in creating man was for man to contain and express Him. But before man took God in, he was tempted by Satan and became fallen. Because of man's fall, God gave the law to expose man's true condition. The law was enacted according to what God is. Hence, the law is a portrait of what God is. If you carefully study the Ten Commandments, you will realize that the essence of the commandments is love, light, holiness, and righteousness. Because God Himself is love, light, holiness, and righteousness, the law that He made is the expression of love, light, holiness, and righteousness.

CHRIST AS THE EMBODIMENT
OF WHAT GOD IS

Due to the fall, man's condition no longer corresponded to that which was portrayed by the law. Therefore, God in Christ had to become a man. In other words, Christ is the God of love, light, holiness, and righteousness who put on man.

In the four Gospels we see that the life which Christ lived on earth may be represented by four words: love, light, holiness, and righteousness. His walk on earth was the expression of love, light, holiness, and righteousness. He became a man to fulfill the law. Therefore, as a real man, He lived God completely. God was fully expressed through Him, and the image of a true man was also manifested, thereby fulfilling, and even exceeding, the requirements of the law.

CHRIST BECOMING THE SPIRIT TO ENTER INTO MAN FOR MAN TO LIVE OUT WHAT CHRIST IS

In order to enter into us to be our life, Christ died for our sins to resolve the problem of our sin and then resurrected from among the dead to become the life-giving Spirit. When Christ enters into us as the life-giving Spirit, it is God entering into us. Since God is love, light, holiness, and righteousness, when He enters into us, it is love, light, holiness, and righteousness entering into us. However, as fallen people, we are corrupt and unclean. Therefore, even though we have a little measure of love, light, holiness, and righteousness within us, it is distorted and deficient. Hence, our expression of Christ is so inadequate. Although we have been saved, we are still so unbecoming. We still need to let Christ grow in us daily that He may be completely lived out through us. Thus, within us Christians, not only do we have God and Christ, but we also have the human virtues that correspond to the law.

In Romans 8:4 Paul said, "That the righteous requirement of the law might be fulfilled in us, who do not walk according to the flesh but according to the spirit." Because all the requirements of the law have been fulfilled in Christ as the life-giving Spirit, when we walk according to the spirit, the righteousness of the law is fulfilled. However, some Christians, even though they have Christ in them, revert to religion just as the Galatians did. Once religion comes in, it confuses people so that instead of the expression of God as love, light, holiness, and righteousness, all they have are rituals, practices of worship, and ordinances. Religion cannot express God; rather, it is a hindrance. Moreover, like the Colossians, some Christians pursue philosophy. Religion plus philosophy bring in even more confusion.

We must be clear that we are not speaking about the moral principles in human relationships commonly taught among the Chinese people. Rather, we are speaking about the biblical virtues that God desires. The virtues that God wants are God Himself lived out through us as love, light, holiness, and righteousness. The morality that we work out is at best that which Paul referred to as "the righteousness which is out of the law" in Philippians 3. We know that before Paul was saved, all he pursued was the righteousness which is out of the law. The ancient Chinese sages taught people to practice filial piety, brotherly subordination, honesty, shamefacedness, benevolence, justice, propriety, and prudence, all of which are tantamount to the righteousness which is in the law that Paul pursued after. Paul pursued the righteousness which is in the law according to the law, whereas the Chinese pursue the morality taught by the ancient sages according to the philosophy concerning human relationships. Both have the same results; both are not what God wants.

Therefore, the virtues that we speak about are the expressions of God in humanity. They are not the ethics taught by the Chinese. Rather, they are Christ revealed in the Bible. Christ is our life within, and He is also our living without. In this way what we live out are our virtues. Therefore, we should use the word *virtues* instead of *ethics*. When we mention ethics, we always correlate it to the conventional ethics taught by Confucius and Mencius. But the virtues of Christians are the expression of God as love, light, holiness, and righteousness.

THE VIRTUES IN THE BOOK OF PHILIPPIANS BEING LOVE, LIGHT, HOLINESS, AND RIGHTEOUSNESS

Philippians 4:8-9 mentions a total of eight virtues. The first six items include the things that are true, the things that are dignified, the things that are righteous, the things that are pure, the things that are lovely, and the things that are well spoken of. The last two items include any virtue and any praise, which are a summary of the first six items. Actually, these six items are just love, light, holiness, and righteousness. That which is lovely is love; that which is righteous is righteousness; that which is pure and well spoken of—that which is honest and upright—is light; that which is true and dignified is holiness. If you carefully analyze these six items, you can categorize them under four big items: love, light, holiness, and righteousness. According to the entire book of Philippians, the things that are true, dignified, pure, righteous, lovely, and well spoken of are the living out of God through us as love, light, holiness, and righteousness. These four items are not only virtuous but also good; hence, they are excellent. The Greek word for *virtue* denotes a lovely condition manifested through struggle and endeavor. Several times in the Chinese Union Version this word is rendered "moral act," implying something powerful and manifesting brightness. This is not the conventional ethics taught by the ancient Chinese sages. Rather, this is God being life in us and expressing what He is—love, light, holiness, and righteousness—according to the image by which He created us.

We were empty vessels created in God's image. Although we had love, light, holiness, and righteousness in our humanity, they were empty because there was no real content. However, after we are saved, Christ fills us as our reality, and He is lived out of us. Thus, the love, light, holiness, and righteousness that we live out are no longer empty virtues; rather, they are virtues that have been enriched by God. This means that God has enriched and magnified the virtues, which include love, light, holiness, and righteousness, in our humanity with His divinity. This is the lovely state that results from the struggling and striving of the divine power within us. This condition is what the Scriptures refer to as virtue.

EXPERIENCING THE TRIUNE GOD
IN THE BOOK OF PHILIPPIANS

In such a short book as the Epistle to the Philippians we can also see the revelation of the Triune God. First, we see "the Spirit of Jesus Christ" (1:19). Today the Holy Spirit is not only the Spirit of God but also the Spirit of Jesus Christ. Second, we see "the power of His [Christ's] resurrection" (3:10a). Christ, the second among the Trinity—the Father, the Son, and the Spirit—is now the resurrected Christ with the power of resurrection. Third, we see the "God of peace" (4:9) operating within us to give us peace. This God who gives us peace is not outside of us but is inside of us. God can only be in us after the resurrection of Christ. The God who is in us is the Father. Therefore, in the book of Philippians we clearly see that first there is the Father, second there is the Son, and third there is the Spirit. The Spirit is the Spirit of Jesus Christ; the Son is the resurrected Christ; and the Father is the God in resurrection as our peace operating, restricting, and guarding within us. This is the Triune God for our experience and enjoyment.

The title of the Divine Trinity—the Father, the Son, and the Holy Spirit—was not clearly disclosed before the resurrection of the Lord Jesus. Although the revelation concerning the Triune God has been implied in many places both in the Old Testament and the New Testament, it still requires human inference. For example, Genesis 1:1 says, "God created the heavens and the earth"; the Hebrew word here for *God* is plural. Then verse 26 says, "And God said, Let Us make man in Our image, according to Our likeness." The God in verse 1 becomes "Us" in verse 26. Hence, by inference, we conclude that God is triune. We still cannot see this clearly in the plain text of the Old Testament. However, when the Lord Jesus resurrected from the dead, He told the disciples, "Go therefore and disciple all the nations, baptizing them into the name of the Father and of the Son and of the Holy Spirit" (Matt 28:19). The process of the Trinity was completed after the resurrection of the Lord Jesus. At that point in time, the Father became the Father in resurrection, the Son became the Son in resurrection, and the Spirit became the Spirit in resurrection. In other words, God is triune, but it was not until after the Lord Jesus resurrected that the Triune God was consummated in the Spirit. After the Lord Jesus resurrected, the Spirit became the life-giving Spirit, the Son became the resurrected Christ, and the Father became the God who indwells man.

We have said that the book of Philippians is a book on the experience of Christ; it speaks about living out Christ in our daily life. Living out Christ in our daily life means that God in Christ enters into us to be our life and reality and that He is expressed through our humanity in our human love, light, holiness, and righteousness. Therefore, this book speaks about how Christ in us becomes our life and how we are empowered to live out Christ. To summarize all that we

have covered previously, we can see that the Spirit of Jesus
Christ is here, the resurrected Christ is here, and the God in
resurrection is here. The Triune God is in us. All three of
Them—the Father, the Son, and the Holy Spirit—are in us.
Yet They are not three Gods but one God. The one God
becomes triune so that we can experience Him. This is truly
a great mystery. It is a mystery that cannot be explained
adequately with human words. This wonderful Triune God
lives in us to be our life and life supply.

EXPERIENCING THE BOUNTIFUL SUPPLY
OF THE SPIRIT OF JESUS CHRIST

Philippians 1:19 refers to "the bountiful supply of the
Spirit of Jesus Christ." The phrase *the Spirit of Jesus Christ*
shows us that Jesus Christ is the Spirit and that the Spirit is
Jesus Christ Himself. When we experience Christ, we experience Him as the Spirit, because Christ can be in us only by
being the Spirit. Therefore, Jesus Christ is truly a wonderful
One. He is God who became a man, Christ who became Jesus,
the One in whom God and man were united and mingled. He
is God and He is also Man. This is Jesus Christ. When He is
experienced by us, He is the Spirit. This Spirit who is in us
is Jesus Christ, the God-man, with the bountiful supply.

Today the Lord Jesus is the Spirit in us, and this Spirit
has a bountiful supply. He supplies whatever we need. Furthermore, this Jesus Christ has the power of resurrection,
and this power is inseparable from the Spirit of Jesus Christ;
the two are one. Concerning His supply, He is the Spirit of
Jesus Christ; concerning His power, He is the resurrected
Christ.

EXPERIENCING THE POWER OF
CHRIST'S RESURRECTION

Ephesians 1:19-20 says, "And what is the surpassing
greatness of His power toward us who believe, according to
the operation of the might of His strength, which He caused
to operate in Christ in raising Him from the dead and seating
Him at His right hand in the heavenlies." The Lord Jesus
was resurrected and released from the detention of death

and the grave. Furthermore, He ascended to heaven and was enthroned. This is the power of His resurrection. Is there any other force in the universe that is greater than the power of resurrection? The Spirit with the bountiful supply, who is in us, has the power of the resurrected Christ.

In Philippians 4:13 Paul said, "I am able to do all things in Him who empowers me." Christ is the One who empowers us. The word *empowers* here and the word *power* in Ephesians 1:19 come from the same Greek word for *dynamic* or *dynamo*. Christ as the source of all power is inexhaustible; His power is unlimitedly great. In the Chinese Union Version, the Greek word for *power* is translated in some places as *great power,* in other places as *strength,* and in still other places as *power*. Regardless of whether it is *great power,* or *strength,* or *power,* we have it because we have Christ in us as the driving force. When the resurrection power of Christ operates in us, we become empowered. Today there are many toys that are electrically powered. For example, there is a toy dog that has batteries installed in it. If the switch is not turned on, the dog cannot move, but when the switch is turned on, the dog begins jumping around. The electricity from the batteries is what empowers the dog. Likewise, without Christ operating in us, we do not have the driving force. When the power of Christ's resurrection operates in us, we are made alive and empowered. Christ is the resurrected One. Once the resurrection power begins to operate in us, it enables us to break through death and transcend everything.

Philippians 2:13 says, "For it is God who operates in you both the willing and the working for His good pleasure." The willing is within; the working is without. When a person has the inward willing, he will have the outward working. Our willing and our working are the result of God's operation in us. The word *operates* may also be rendered *energizes,* which is derived from the Greek word *ergon*. This word does not mean to operate outwardly; it means to energize from within. The Spirit with the bountiful supply and the Christ of resurrection are God Himself who operates and energizes in us both the willing and the working for His good pleasure.

EXPERIENCING GOD'S GUARDING US IN CHRIST

God not only energizes us within but also guards and protects our hearts and our thoughts. We have a great deal of worries in our mind. Perhaps we are able to temporarily set aside our worries at night when we go to sleep, but as soon as we wake up, our mind begins turning again. We worry about our job, our business, our health, our homework, and many other things, so that our whole being is full of anxiety and without peace. But Philippians 4:7 says that the peace of God, which surpasses every man's understanding, guards and protects us. This peace is God Himself. When we have outward difficulties, God guards us from within so that our hearts are not troubled.

We who are lovers of the Lord can testify that many times problems come to us and we do not know what to do, yet if we would just turn our hearts to the Lord and offer praise and thanksgiving to Him, immediately there is an unspeakable peace that calms us so that we do not have any anxiety. Without peace, we cannot enter into the enjoyment of Christ. Hence, we must let God be the peace in us to guard our hearts and our thoughts. This is what the resurrected Christ is doing in us today. As the God of peace, He not only operates and energizes in us but also guards and protects our mind that we may have peace in our entire being. In this way we can then enter into Christ to enjoy Him.

THE SUBJECTIVE SALVATION
OF THE TRIUNE GOD

In summary, the Triune God is in us not only as our life but also as our bountiful supply. Moreover, He is the power that overcomes death. He has ascended from Hades into the third heaven, far above all rule and authority. This power empowers us from within; moreover, the resurrected God operates in us and energizes us. Our thoughts and actions come from His energizing us within. When we have difficulties, He guards and protects our mind so that we can enjoy peace. A person who truly loves the Lord and lives in the Lord must necessarily be a man of peace. Although he is troubled with a lot of difficulties outwardly, he has the inner peace. In such a peaceful state of mind, what he lives out is love, light, holiness, and righteousness. This is God in Christ expressed in human virtues.

The subjective salvation of the Triune God is greatly different from human ethics. Human ethics teach us merely to have good behavior, but what we are speaking about is God being lived out in our humanity as love, light, holiness, and righteousness. When we live out these virtues, God is expressed. This is what Paul said, "For to me, to live is Christ," which also means that "as always, even now Christ will be magnified in my body." These words are not mere doctrines or exhortations but a revelation of the truth for us to truly know that the salvation which we have received is the Triune God being our enjoyment and experience in our daily living and becoming our subjective salvation.

CHAPTER NINE

HOW TO ENJOY THE SUBJECTIVE SALVATION OF THE TRIUNE GOD

Scripture Reading: Phil. 1:19-20; 3:10; 4:13; 2:12-13; 4:6, 9

In this chapter we want to see how to enjoy the subjective salvation of the Triune God which we covered in the previous chapter. We especially use the word *enjoy* because enjoying is higher than experiencing. We not only experience but even more enjoy the subjective salvation of the Triune God.

MAN BEING A VESSEL CREATED BY GOD TO CONTAIN HIM

The Bible reveals that man is a vessel created by God to contain Him. Our body needs to be satisfied with the outward physical things, such as food, clothing, shelter, and transportation. Our soul also needs to be satisfied with some form of relaxation and entertainment. The outer part of man is the body, which belongs to the physical realm. Within the body is the soul, which belongs to the psychological realm, and within the soul is the spirit, which is the innermost part of man. Many people have satisfied their need for food, clothing, shelter, and transportation, and they also have found solace and happiness in their soul, yet they are still empty and unsatisfied deep within their spirit. The spirit of man, which is the deepest part of man, is his true "I," his true self.

A large part of man's spirit is his conscience. People often say that they speak according to their conscience. This means that they speak according to their true "I." Whenever when we argue with others, we always say we are right. This is to speak from our soul. However, in the midst of our reasoning something deep within tells us, "No, you are wrong." Sometimes our intellect allows us to do a certain thing and our emotion also delights in doing it, yet our deepest part, which possesses an innate ability to distinguish right and wrong, tells us, "That is wrong. Don't do it." This innate ability to distinguish right and wrong is actually our conscience, which is part of the spirit in man. Just as man's body and soul have their own needs, so man's spirit also has its needs. Because of the need that is in man's spirit, man invented religion. What the spirit of man needs is to worship and contain God.

Human history throughout the ages contains records of the worship of God both among the barbaric nations and civilized societies. The barbaric nations worship God in a wild way, whereas the civilized people worship God in a refined way. The objects of worship of the barbaric nations are lowly; their idols are crudely made. The objects of worship of the civilized nations are noble; their idols are fine and exquisite. The higher the civilization, the higher the worship. This is similar to saying that the higher the culture, the more particular the food. Therefore, there are inferior religions and there are also superior religions; there are backward religions and there are also advanced religions.

RELIGION VERSUS GOD'S PURPOSE

Religion is the most noble thing in the entire human culture. We may say that without religion, the human race becomes barbaric. Religion indeed occupies a high position in human culture. Man drinks because he is thirsty. Man eats because he is hungry. Man puts on clothing to keep himself warm. Then, why does man need religion? Because man's innermost part has a need. Religion meets that need in man. We eat and drink to satisfy the needs of our body, but religion is to satisfy man's inner need. The Chinese people say that man has four basic needs: food, clothing, shelter, and transportation. These needs, which are all outward, do not comprise all the needs of our human life. We human beings are not simple. Not only do we have a body, but we also have a spirit and a soul. The soul is what we commonly refer to as our psyche. Some people have fully satisfied their need for food, clothing, shelter, and transportation; however, they still have their psychological needs. They listen to music, watch dramas, and read books and newspapers to be refreshed and comforted. However, after they have met their psychological needs, they are still not satisfied because they still have a spirit within them that has its need.

Many people have achieved success and acquired fame and prominence. In man's eyes, they should have no lack at all; they can have whatever they want. However, they are still not satisfied because the need in their spirit has not yet been satisfied. Although they have no lack physically and psychologically, their innermost part still has a need that can be satisfied only by the Creator of heaven and earth. This is because man was created for God, for the purpose of containing God.

In Chinese, the term *religion* literally means to have an object of worship and teach accordingly. Man worships God and teaches according to what he worships. This is religion. In brief, religion presents God for people to worship and exhorts them to do good according to the God whom they worship. The crudeness or refinement in the practice of a religion varies according to the degree of civilization and the status and qualifications of the individual, but the principle is the same. Because most people consider Christianity a refined and high-class religion, when they read the Bible, they consider the Bible to be a religious book. They think that the Bible teaches people to worship God and to do good accordingly. Today thousands of Christians cannot divorce themselves from this kind of thinking. When they read the Bible, they consider the Bible to be a book that presents an object for worship and teaches people to do good. Actually, doing good according to the object of one's worship is not the truth in the universe.

The truth in the universe is that there is only one true God, the Creator of all things. He created man with a particular purpose that man may express Him. In order for man to attain to this purpose, God must enter into man to become man's life so that man may live out God. This universal truth does not exist in any religion even though it is very clearly recorded in the Bible. Moreover, the majority of Christians have lost this truth. Because Christianity has become a religion, our attitude should be that we care only for Christ and not for Christianity. We only want Christ; we do not want the rituals, letters, traditions, and regulations of Christianity. This statement may puzzle some people. They may wonder how we can say that we do not want worship meetings, traditions, or rituals and that we only want Christ. Indeed, this is very difficult to comprehend, but we still declare that we only preach Christ; we do not preach Christianity.

GOD CREATING MAN WITH A SPIRIT
THAT MAN MAY CONTACT AND RECEIVE HIM

The Bible tells us that in the universe there is only one sovereign Lord. This fact is undeniable. It has been proven by science, by your heart, and by the need which is in your spirit that there is one unique sovereign Lord in the universe. You may call Him Jehovah; you may call Him Jesus; you may call Him the Triune God; you may also call Him the Lord of heaven and earth, the God of all things. He is the origin of the universe and the source of all things.

God created all things in the universe for man. The heavens are for the earth, and the earth is for man. If there were no heavens, then there would be no sunlight, air, or rain, and the living things would not grow. These things are for the earth and for the men on earth. Thank the Lord that the earth produces everything we need for our existence. The earth produces all the things that our bodies need. Therefore, the heavens are for the earth, and the earth is for man. Man's living on earth is not meaningless. Man was created for God. Therefore, God created man with a spirit that man may contact and receive Him. God is Spirit, and those who contact Him must contact Him in spirit. Just as only metals can conduct electricity, so only the spirit can communicate with the Spirit.

In order to contact God in spirit, sometimes we have to stop the activities of our body and our soul, and then we have to cry out to God and call on the Lord Jesus from our deepest part. If we do this, immediately there will be light within us. Whenever we stop the activities of our body and our soul, allow the Spirit to work in us, and call from our spirit,

"O God! O Lord Jesus," then, instead of being in our outward activities, we remain in our spirit, the innermost part of our being. At that moment, we know for sure that the existence of God is a reality. This may be compared to breathing. You may not feel that air exists, but it is very convenient for us to enjoy air today. We neither sense that air is here nor feel that we need it. However, when we are deprived of air, we begin to realize that air is real. Just as our body needs air, so our spirit needs God. Therefore, the Bible says that our life and breath depend on Him (Job 12:10). Our physical body needs air; without air, there is no life. Likewise, God is man's true breath. Therefore, when the Lord Jesus came to His disciples after His resurrection, He did not charge them to be zealous, instruct Peter to change his quick disposition, or ask John to listen to Peter. The Lord came to the disciples to breathe into them that they might receive the Holy Spirit, the holy breath (John 20:22). The Holy Spirit is the life-giving Spirit, and the holy breath is the breath of life. Consequently, the disciples received the life of God.

WORSHIPPING GOD, WHO IS SPIRIT, IN SPIRIT AND TRUTHFULNESS

God is our spiritual life. We have a spirit in us, and God wants us to use our spirit to contact Him, and not only to contact Him but to receive Him. The more we contact Him, the more we receive Him, and the more we receive Him, the more we have life. Religion teaches us according to what we worship. However, this is not what the Bible teaches. The Bible tells us that we must receive God as our life. The Samaritan woman in John 4 was a religionist, yet she had no satisfaction. She had sinned and had changed husbands five times, and even the one whom she had at the time was not her husband. However, the Lord Jesus did not rebuke her. Instead, He told her to bring her husband to Him. As soon as the matter of her husband was brought up, the woman's conscience was touched. Immediately she tried to avoid the issue by asking some religious questions. The Lord Jesus turned her back to her spirit and showed her that man worships God neither on Mount Gerizim in Samaria nor on Mount Zion in

Jerusalem. The worship that God desires is in the human spirit.

We must be in spirit and receive Christ as truthfulness; only then can our worship of God be true, real, and not empty. John 4:24 says, "God is Spirit, and those who worship Him must worship in spirit and truthfulness." We must worship God with Christ as truthfulness. The Bible does not speak about religion; it speaks about God. God did not come to teach but to enter into us to be our life. This is the fundamental truth in the Bible. We are not preaching a religion, nor are we trying to make ourselves different from others. We only preach the truth because, by the mercy of God, we have seen the truth in the Bible. Not only are the Gentile religions futile, but even Judaism and Christianity, including Catholicism, are useless. All religions are empty; only Christ Himself is reality. Christ is the embodiment of God; He is God. To receive Christ is to receive God. This is the true worship towards God.

If we see this, it will be a great help to our enjoyment of the subjective salvation of the Triune God. The Bible does not teach us how to behave. Rather, it tells us to enjoy the Triune God—the Father, the Son, and the Spirit. The Triune God is neither a doctrine nor a designation in theology; rather, the Triune God is to be received as our life that He may become our enjoyment. The Bible shows us that God is our food, our living water, and our spiritual breath; all these are for our enjoyment. No one ever says that he has to experience eating. Eating is not an experience but an enjoyment. God saves us not only for us to experience His salvation but also for us to enjoy Him.

THE TRIUNE GOD
NOT FOR OUR DOCTRINAL UNDERSTANDING
BUT FOR OUR ENJOYMENT

The Triune God—the Father, the Son, and the Spirit—is a mystery. The Father, the Son, and the Spirit as the Three in One are not for our doctrinal understanding of theology but for our enjoyment. God has to be the Father, the Son, and the Spirit so that He can work Himself into us. I met in the

Brethren Assembly for many years, and the teachers there told me, "When you pray, you should not pray to the Spirit. The most accurate way of prayer is to pray to the Father, in the name of the Son, by the precious blood of the Son, and through the moving of the Spirit." Therefore, I tried to pray carefully according to their instructions. Sometimes, if I made a mistake due to carelessness, I had to confess my sins and rectify my error. Gradually, I checked my own experience and realized that that was not right. However, the Brethren teachers said that the heavenly Father is in heaven, the Son is sitting beside the heavenly Father, and the Spirit is sent to us. They were not very clear, however, about who the Spirit is. If you read the King James Version of the Bible, you will see that Romans 8:16 uses the pronoun *itself* to refer to the Spirit, yet *itself* is a pronoun that refers to a thing. Over three hundred years ago in the translation of the King James Version, the most authoritative English version, the translators considered the Spirit to be a power, a thing, but not a person. In the recent one hundred years when other versions were being translated, the translators changed the pronoun *itself* to *Himself,* acknowledging that the Holy Spirit is indeed a person.

God the Father made a plan. God the Son came to be among mankind through incarnation and accomplished the great work of God's redemption by His death on the cross. After He accomplished redemption, He entered into resurrection. In resurrection, as the last Adam, He became the life-giving Spirit. He had to become the life-giving Spirit in order to enter into us. When the Lord Jesus was on the earth, He was with the disciples for three and a half years, and the disciples enjoyed His presence. However, one day the Lord suddenly told them that He was going away. He also said that it was expedient for them that He go away, because if He did not go away, He could only be in their midst, but He could not enter into them. Therefore, He had to go away that another Comforter might be sent to them. This other Comforter was the Spirit of reality as the transfiguration of the first Comforter. The first One was in the flesh; the other One was the first

One transfigured as the Spirit of reality. When the Spirit of reality came, He entered into them to be their life.

Today, God is not only the Father and the Son, but He is also the Spirit. He is not only the Father who planned in eternity. He is also the Son who in the flesh accomplished God's plan. Now He is the Spirit who brings and applies to us what the Father planned and what the Son accomplished. The Spirit as the consummation of the Triune God is now in us to be our life for our enjoyment.

ENJOYING THE SUBJECTIVE SALVATION
OF THE TRIUNE GOD

We need to enjoy the Triune God, and we need the subjective salvation of the Triune God; we do not need religion. We do not need to work out something for ourselves or to reform our behavior; we need to enjoy the Triune God. The Triune God is the consummated Spirit, and He is also Christ, who is God Himself. Now we want to see the way to enjoy the subjective salvation of the Triune God through the verses in the book of Philippians. These verses cover three main points: first concerning the Spirit, second concerning Christ, and third concerning God.

The Bountiful Supply
of the Spirit of Jesus Christ

Philippians 1:19 says, "For I know that for me this will turn out to salvation through your petition and the bountiful supply of the Spirit of Jesus Christ." The second half of verse 20 goes on to say, "But with all boldness, as always, even now Christ will be magnified in my body, whether through life or through death." These two verses contain profound meanings. According to the context, we see that the Spirit of Jesus Christ is Christ Himself because the bountiful supply of the Spirit of Jesus Christ enables us to magnify Christ. The bountiful supply of the Spirit of Jesus Christ is for Christ to be magnified; therefore, the magnified Christ is the Spirit of Jesus Christ.

The bountiful supply of the Spirit of Jesus Christ is in us, but do we magnify Christ? The secret to the enjoyment of the bountiful supply of the Spirit of Jesus Christ is to magnify Christ. For example, there can be a sumptuous feast before me, but if I refuse to move my hands or open my mouth, then the abundant supply has nothing to do with me. Likewise, God has a rich supply completely prepared for us, and He is inviting us to come to the feast. Are we willing to accept His invitation and come to dine at the feast? The bountiful supply of the Spirit of Jesus Christ is the riches of the gospel; the entire gospel is incorporated in the Spirit of Jesus Christ (Gal. 3:14). The riches of the gospel are not only in the Bible but also in the Spirit. Today, God works through the Holy Bible and by the Holy Spirit. The Bible is the clear word with black letters printed on white paper; the Holy Spirit is the living reality in our spirit. We have the Holy Bible, and we also have the Holy Spirit. What we preach is the content of the gospel, and the Holy Spirit has a bountiful supply, which is also the content of the gospel. However, it is not enough merely to have the bountiful supply as the content of the gospel; we must still eat. It is by our eating that Christ may be magnified in our body.

The truth in the Bible is different from the teaching of religion. Religion teaches people to do good and encourages them to do it by themselves. But it is not so with the Bible. The truth in the Bible is that the bountiful supply of God is available through the words of the Bible and through the Spirit of Jesus Christ. You are not required to do any work; rather, you just need to receive and enjoy. The bountiful supply of Jesus Christ is here. What matters now is that you enjoy Him and allow Him to be magnified.

The Power of the Resurrection of Christ

Philippians 3:10 says, "To know Him and the power of His resurrection." The power of resurrection is the content of the bountiful supply of the Spirit of Jesus Christ. The bountiful supply is the power of resurrection. The two are synonyms; both refer to the same thing. Without the resurrection power, the bountiful supply is empty. Then, 4:13 tells us the way to enjoy the bountiful supply. This verse says, "I am able to do all things in Him who empowers me." Christ is powerful; He has the power of resurrection. You must be in Him to enjoy His bountiful supply in power. However, too often you are not in Him. Although you have believed in the Lord Jesus, you are not in Him but rather in your mind, in your thoughts, and in your flesh. Therefore, it is not possible for you to enjoy His bountiful supply. Christ is the all-inclusive, life-giving Spirit, dispensing all His riches into us. Hence, we need to remain in our mingled spirit to enjoy all His supply.

God Operating in Us

Philippians 2:13 says, "For it is God who operates in you both the willing and the working for His good pleasure." The willing is within; the working is without. The willing takes place in our will, indicating that God's operation begins from our spirit (cf. 4:23) and spreads into our mind, emotion, and will. As a Christian, you have God operating in you. What you need is to cooperate with Him by obeying Him. However He moves, you just obey. Do not make up your mind to not lose your temper again; this is futile. If you do not make up your mind, you probably will not lose your temper. However, once you make up your mind, you can be assured that you will lose your temper. You have to realize that there is no way to reform yourself. God does not want you to reform yourself; He wants you to enjoy Him. Today, God is the life-giving Spirit with a bountiful supply, and He wants to enter into you to operate in you. You must cease all your activities and let Him work in you.

Philippians 4:6 says, "In nothing be anxious, but in everything, by prayer and petition with thanksgiving, let your requests be made known to God." Prayer is general, having worship and fellowship as its essence; petition is special, being for particular needs. We should tell God of all that we want. Some people might say, "I tell God, but He does not answer." This is because they want things outside of God. God never answers this kind of prayer. Of course, I cannot represent God to tell you that He will never answer this kind of prayer, but my experience has been that it is irrelevant whether or not He answers this kind of prayer. I can testify that if He desires to give you something, He will give it to you whether or not you pray for it; if He does not want to give it to you, you will never receive it even if you pray for it. This is because the Lord said, "Therefore do not be anxious, saying, What shall we eat? or, What shall we drink? or, With what shall we be clothed?...But seek first His kingdom and His righteousness, and all these things will be added to you" (Matt. 6:31, 33).

We should pray for such matters as our not having spiritual growth, our being short of the divine life, our not living an overcoming life, our not walking according to the Spirit, and our not living Christ. Moreover, we need to pray with thanksgiving. Instead of begging, we should pray and petition with thanksgiving. To pray with thanksgiving means that although your request has not yet been answered, you believe that you have already received it. You have faith that God will grant you what you have asked for. The result of this kind of fellowship with God in prayer is seen in Philippians 4:7: "And the peace of God, which surpasses every man's understanding, will guard your hearts and your thoughts in Christ Jesus."

THE WAY TO ENJOY
THE SUBJECTIVE SALVATION OF THE TRIUNE GOD
BEING TO COOPERATE WITH HIM

The way to experience the subjective salvation of the Triune God is to cooperate with Him. He has the bountiful supply, but you have to allow Him to supply you. He has power, but you have to be in Him. If you are not in Him, even if He has the bountiful supply and the resurrection power, they cannot be your enjoyment. Furthermore, He is operating in you, but you have to cooperate with Him and obey Him. The best expression of obedience is prayer. A proper prayer is always accompanied with thanksgiving. This means you need to pray and petition with thanksgiving. Consequently, God can operate in you to protect your inner man and guard your heart and your thoughts. In this way you will enjoy His peace and presence.

In conclusion, we need to cooperate with God. He has the bountiful supply, but we need to cooperate with Him. In other words, we need to submit to His moving within us, and we also need to pray and petition with thanksgiving. When we do this, immediately we will sense that He is operating within us and guarding us. Not only is He protecting us outwardly, but He is also guarding our hearts and our thoughts. Thus, we enjoy the subjective salvation of the Triune God. When we have this kind of enjoyment, what we live out is Christ being magnified in our body.

You have to go before the Lord and pray, "Lord, I thank You that You are the rich Spirit, who is all-inclusive and supplying bountifully. I thank You also that You are the resurrected Lord with the power of resurrection. Lord, I thank You even more that You are the God of peace who gives me peace. I want to stop all my activities; I will no longer struggle, strive, or expect to change myself. Lord, I do not want to love the world or the things that are outside of You. I just love You; I love You in singleness of heart. Lord, thank You that, as the Triune God, You are operating within me. I desire to cooperate with You to enjoy Your bountiful supply and experience Your resurrection power in me. Much more, every moment I desire to pray and petition with thanksgiving and make known to You all the things that I desire concerning being spiritual, sanctified, and victorious." Dear brothers and sisters, if you pray in this manner, you will have peace within you, and immediately you will enjoy the presence and the operation of God within you. You will truly sense that there is a power supporting you. This is enjoyment. Do not wait until a prayer time to have this enjoyment; you need to maintain a prayerful spirit the entire day.

This is why the Bible tells us to pray unceasingly. If we remain in a prayerful spirit, then we will continuously enjoy the Triune God. Today, the Triune God—the Father in the Son as the Spirit—has imparted into us all that He has accomplished, all that He is, and all that He can do. Today, we need to cooperate with Him, to obey Him, and to let Him work within us; moreover, we need to pray and petition always with thanksgiving and to speak to Him always in a prayerful spirit. Then, we will enjoy Him as life and peace. This is the enjoyment of the subjective salvation of the Triune God.

ABOUT THE AUTHOR

Witness Lee was born in 1905 in northern China and raised in a Christian family. At age 19 he was fully captured for Christ and immediately consecrated himself to preach the gospel for the rest of his life. Early in his service, he met Watchman Nee, a renowned preacher, teacher, and writer. Witness Lee labored together with Watchman Nee under his direction. In 1934 Watchman Nee entrusted Witness Lee with the responsibility for his publication operation, called the Shanghai Gospel Bookroom.

Prior to the Communist takeover in 1949, Witness Lee was sent by Watchman Nee and his other co-workers to Taiwan to ensure that the things delivered to them by the Lord would not be lost. Watchman Nee instructed Witness Lee to continue the former's publishing operation abroad as the Taiwan Gospel Bookroom, which has been publicly recognized as the publisher of Watchman Nee's works outside China. Witness Lee's work in Taiwan manifested the Lord's abundant blessing. From a mere 350 believers, newly fled from the mainland, the churches in Taiwan grew to 20,000 in five years.

In 1962 Witness Lee felt led of the Lord to come to the United States, settling in California. During his 35 years of service in the U.S., he ministered in weekly meetings and weekend conferences, delivering several thousand spoken messages. Much of his speaking has since been published as over 400 titles. Many of these have been translated into over fourteen languages. He gave his last public conference in February 1997 at the age of 91.

He leaves behind a prolific presentation of the truth in the Bible. His major work, *Life-study of the Bible,* comprises over 25,000 pages of commentary on every book of the Bible from the perspective of the believers' enjoyment and experience of God's divine life in Christ through the Holy Spirit. Witness Lee was the chief editor of a new translation of the New Testament into Chinese called the Recovery Version and directed the translation of the same into English. The Recovery Version also appears in a number of other languages. He provided an extensive body of footnotes, outlines, and spiritual cross references. A radio broadcast of his messages can be heard on Christian radio stations in the United States. In 1965 Witness Lee founded Living Stream Ministry, a non-profit corporation, located in Anaheim, California, which officially presents his and Watchman Nee's ministry.

Witness Lee's ministry emphasizes the experience of Christ as life and the practical oneness of the believers as the Body of Christ. Stressing the importance of attending to both these matters, he led the churches under his care to grow in Christian life and function. He was unbending in his conviction that God's goal is not narrow sectarianism but the Body of Christ. In time, believers began to meet simply as the church in their localities in response to this conviction. In recent years a number of new churches have been raised up in Russia and in many eastern European countries.